Questions

of

Heaven

THE CONCORD LIBRARY
Series Editor: John Elder

Questions

of

Heaven

THE CHINESE JOURNEYS
OF AN AMERICAN BUDDHIST

Gretel Ehrlich

BEACON

PRESS

BOSTON

BEACON PRESS
25 Beacon Street
Boston, Massachusetts 02108-2892

BEACON PRESS BOOKS
are published under the auspices of
the Unitarian Universalist Association of Congregations.

02 01 00 99 98   8 7 6 5 4 3 2

Text design by Anne Chalmers
Composition by Wilsted & Taylor

Credits can be found on page 127.

Library of Congress Cataloging-in-Publication Data
can be found on page 129.

Why climb a mountain?

Look! a mountain there.

I don't climb mountain.
Mountain climbs me.
Mountain is myself.
I climb on myself.

There is no mountain
nor myself.
Something
moves up and down
in the air.

—Nanao Sakaki

Contents

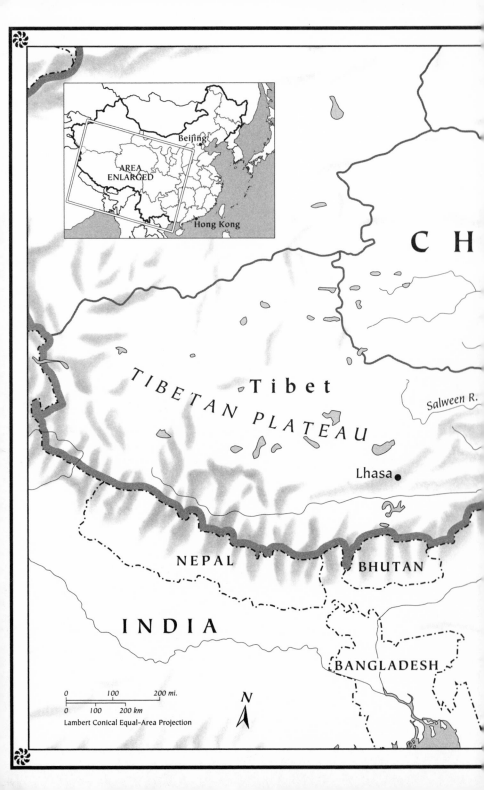

Questions

of

Heaven

1

THE

ROAD

TO

EMEI SHAN

MAY 1995. Sichuan Province, western China.

All afternoon Mr. Tong, my driver, has been navigating his polished land cruiser through labyrinthian Chinese traffic. We are making our way south from the city of Chengdu in the province of Sichuan, to Emei Shan, one of China's four sacred Buddhist mountains, which I have come to climb. From the Min River valley, Emei Shan's 10,167-foot peak is obscured from view by reefs of black coal dust and gray smog mixed with rain clouds. High up on its slopes, winter snows are still melting and the summer monsoons that cause these wide rivers to flood have not yet begun. In his plum-colored nylon jacket and dark aviator glasses, Mr. Tong's suave handsomeness is movie star material. His high cheekbones, slicked-back hair, and world-weary look bespeak a deep calm no amount of urban chaos—honking horns, foot traffic, rickshaws, bicyclists with pig carcasses slumped over the handlebars, or overloaded donkey carts— can penetrate.

Like most middle-aged Chinese men and women, Mr. Tong endured unspeakable suffering during Mao's despotic regime, which began with the Communist Party takeover in 1949 and intensified during the Cultural Revolution from 1966 to 1977, finally ending with Deng Xiaoping's return to power in 1978. During Liberation Mr. Tong was sent to cadre school, actually a work reform camp, for four years. At the end of his training he wisely refused the rank of cadre, asking instead to be made a driver. Wisely, because he witnessed the executions of class-mates who accepted leadership rank and were later branded as counterrevolutionaries. Mr. Tong's savvy had kept him alive then, so that driving across the Tibetan plateau to Lhasa or tak-ing six hours to go 150 miles now didn't begin to seem like a problem.

We made our way in fits and starts down a highway whose two lanes had turned into five, with no center divide and no rules about how to get from one end of a tangled intersection to the other. Sitting high up in the back seat of Mr. Tong's land-cruiser, I clutched a sheaf of pages brought from home: poems from the *Ch'u ci—Songs of the South—*written in the second century A.D., as well as reproductions of Sung and Ming Dy-nasty landscape paintings. Out the window a sawmill flew by, then a sewing factory, a brick factory, and a group of old men in bamboo chairs sitting around a table playing mah-jongg. I looked down, thumbing through the pages, moving from poems to paintings, and back to poems again, trying to assure myself that these cultural artifacts had been made here.

I turned to a favorite poem from Qu Yuan's erotic shaman songs in the *Ch'u ci*:

> I bathe in orchid water,
> wash my hair with scents,
> put on colored robes,
> flower-figured.
> The spirit twisting and turning . . .

Mr. Tong looked in the rearview mirror. He was trying to see what I was reading, so I passed my handful of poems and paintings forward. He glanced down, shrugged, smiled, and kept driving, as if to say, if that's what you came to China for, you're a thousand years too late.

My map of southwestern China showed a land that might have been clawed by a huge hand. Between those marks, great rivers flowed and writhing cordilleras were staircases descending from the Himalayan roof to low, tropical plateaus swept by monsoons as if the weight of China's 1.2 billion people had pulverized the land into something flat.

We crossed a sinuous river and descended into the heartland of China, the Yangtze River valley, a region once known as Chu. The early poems written there were rhapsodic, erotic, and elegiac; they came out of a region that was wild, semitropical, and full of "barbarians." The author, Qu Yuan, served the local king as a minister but was betrayed by his colleagues, and banished to Chu. After writing the *Songs of Chu*, he drowned himself in a tributary of the Yangtze.

I turned to his long poem *Li Sao*, or, *Encountering Sorrow*:

> Ling Fen had already told me his auspicious augury;
> I would choose a lucky day and commence my
>   journey.
> I broke a branch of carnelian to serve as food
> pounded carnelian fragments to make rations for
>   the road.
> I had flying dragons to draw my vehicle . . .

Out my window I saw no dragons, only a sameness that spread everywhere as if nothing had come before in this country and nothing would change in the future. The buildings were Stalinesque: brutal and banal, and the farms that stretched as far as the eye could see, once feudal fiefs converted by Mao into immense communes, had been broken back down into private domains too poor and small to confer much wealth on the peasant farmer.

I had come to China to pick up the threads of a once flourishing Buddhist culture and thought I could find it in their sacred mountains. Beginning in the west I would climb Emei Shan, to be followed by Putuo Shan, an island off Shanghai, Jiuhua Shan in Anhui Province, and Wutai Shan, northwest of Beijing. Years before, in midwinter, I had roamed the mountains of Japan's northern Honshu, at times following the poet Bashō's trail, kneeling in the spot under a thousand-year-old cypress tree where he and his companion, Sora, had unrolled their blankets and spent the night. In the pilgrim village of Haguro, I was given traditional straw sandals, walked to the top of the mountain in deep snow, drank sacred sake and witnessed celebrations of the New Year during which food and water were blessed.

But this was a China whose religious infrastructure had been ripped apart by the Communist Party during Mao's regime, whose monasteries and temples had been defaced, burned, or demolished, whose monks and nuns had been imprisoned, tortured or killed (and still are in Tibet), and whose culture had been erased. Yet I hoped I could pick up a scent.

I glanced again at the exquisitely balanced paintings of sacred mountains with names like, *Listening to Wind in Pines, Pavilions in Spring Mountains,* and *Mountain Retreat,* then turned to Marco Polo's *Travels.* By the time Marco Polo journeyed through in 1271, China's human population was bulging. There were ten-story buildings and resplendent gardens in such cities as Hangzhou. Papermaking, printing, and published literature—both poetry and prose—music, silk production, advanced medical practices, and slavery all flourished. It was a country where overpopulation was already the norm.

No map can describe the density of human life here, or its effects on the air, water, and land. Western China, the borderland between the Chinese Han people and the Tibet Autonomous Region where twenty of China's fifty-two minority groups live, is knotted with big mountains: Gongga Shan, Yulongxues Shan, Jizu Shan, and Shibao Shan. From these high aeries, big rivers—the Litang Qu, Yalong Jiang, Min Jiang, the Salween, Mekong, and the Yangtze—flow through broad valleys that have been intensively farmed for three thousand years.

The Han Chinese do not seem to be descended from any other peoples. "We rose up from this land. We are autochthonous," a Chinese scholar told me. Their version of origins had no drifting continents bumping into other continents, no migrations of peoples from other places. China had always existed and humans were preponderant. If there was a progenitor, it was Pan Ku, a legendary human who pushed heaven and earth apart to make a space for humans to live. He ruled for eighteen thousand years and after death, his remains made up the sacred mountains of China: his head became the four peaks, his eyes were the sun and moon, his fat was the river and seas, his hair was the grasses and trees.

I could not see Emei Shan or any other high peak out the car window. The roads were not open passageways to a mountain sanctuary, but moving streams of humanity, processionals of farmer-merchants and merchant-peasants in this burgeoning post-Communist marketplace. They carried loads of bricks, bamboo, gravel, cement, rice straw, lumber, dead ducks, coal, live chickens, and caged snakes. Human beings pulled other human beings in rickshaws. These scenes were by no means new to China whose civilization has existed continuously for five thousand years.

My friend Raoul Birnbaum, a Chinese scholar and Buddhist practitioner, had warned me: "The opacities of Chinese culture are difficult to dissolve." So were the obscurations of population and pollution. What Raoul really wanted to say was, "Don't bother to go there, you'll never pick up the thread."

Admittedly, the impetus for the journey had been an idealistic one. In 1991, I'd flown to New York from Wyoming to see an exhibition at the Metropolitan Museum of Art called *Sacred Mountains in Chinese Art*. It was my chance to see the finest medieval landscape paintings that had survived the many dynastic violences of China. I had always loved those scrolls because of the diminutive way humans are tucked into the vertical folds of mountains and because I saw myself there. I had always loved living in the mountains.

Now, bumping through frenzied Chinese traffic, I remembered the January morning I'd left my ranch. A sweeping ground blizzard had flattened my backyard view of mountains rising straight up and had wiped the ground clean. I'd been reading about Sung Dynasty brush styles and inks: the airplane was the painter's brush hovering over a blank scroll, unwinding white to white, putting its tip down here and there to make a mark on the nothingness below.

Shan shui: mountains and waters. In China mountains are not considered whole unless they are conjoined with water. Such is the obsession with mountains that these two words, *shan* and *shui*, refer not only to landscape painting with its companion poems, but also to the whole of China as a nation. But the meaning went deeper: the mountain was a mirror and any itinerary up its paths was a diagram of spiritual progress. Nor was the mountain a single, simple place. It was a center of power whose weathers and textures kept changing, a trope for ongoing transformation.

At the Met I stood before a Han Dynasty Boshan censer—an incense burner shaped like a mountain. A naked man sat on an ox in the center of a pool of water. He held up a mountain with his hand.

In the hot afternoon Mr. Tong drove slowly and surely, his hair unmussed, a biography of a Taiwanese movie star resting on the dashboard. Though we had long since passed out of the city of Chengdu, there was nothing that resembled what Americans think of as countryside. The numbers of people did not diminish: the only change was the kind of work being done. Brick making gave over to rice planting. We passed through clamorous, hellish suburbs and towns, one after another, that gave onto broad farming valleys permeated by the stench of soft coal burning in kitchens and reheated rapeseed oil long since gone rancid, of unregulated streams of raw sewage and the glaze of night soil dippered out over thousands of square miles of intensively farmed land. There was no vista where one could not see the hard labors of water oxen, of peasant women bent under baskets of rice seedlings, of men slogging through leech-glutted mud behind wooden plows. Where farms gave way to sprawling centerless towns, there were unending tableaux of lives and commerce each in their separate bays: rows and rows of tiny shops opened to dusty streets where the sound of local opera blaring from radios was drowned out by the incessant honking of horns.

Yu shan: mountain wandering. That's what I told Mr. Tong I'd come to do. Again, he laughed. Not at me, but for me. He knew all too well how difficult it is to move around in China. He was one of the privileged ones with the use of a government-owned car and special passes that allowed him to travel between certain provinces.

As we inched through heavy traffic I tried to register all that came into my eyes. The poetry of China had always been about traveling, exile, and longing. I wondered what its future subjects now would be. Mr. Tong hummed a traditional mountain tune called a *shan ge*, sung by lovers—one on one mountain, one on the other, with the long melodic dialogues echoing across valleys between—Chinese-style yodeling. What he called Chinese yodelling. He had no reason not to be happy. He was a free man in a Draconian country.

After a while I rested my eyes. Qu Yuan's most difficult poem in the *Songs of Ch'u* is called *Tian Wen*, or *Questions of Heaven*. It is a long series of questions about the origin of the universe, the human condition, and the movements of the planets, sun, and stars. It can be thought of as a series of riddles or koans based on Chinese mythology about why we are what we are, how the cosmos came into being, and what it makes of us. It can also be seen as a table of topics suitable for mythmakers and storytellers. It asks what it was like even before the beginnings of the universe—the same questions being asked by physicists now.

I opened my eyes in time to see a mock Statue of Liberty in an abandoned park and under it, ten men pushing a handcart laden with cement slabs. China once revered a mythical mountain called Mount Kunlun. It rose out of the west and was regarded as the source of all life, the place where "the ten thousand things have their origins and where yin and yang alternate with each other forever." Mountains were thought to connect heaven with earth, spirit with body. A mountain was a pole, an axis mundi, central and vigorous, up which all aspirants shinnied toward enlightenment and slid down towards samsara (human suffering) which are the same.

Guideways through Mountains and Seas (Shan Hai Jing),
written sometime between 480 and 222 B.C., is the first recorded evidence of mountain worship. Twelve chapters are
devoted to descriptions of mountains and their spirit-beings,
which were potent and dangerous: "In the Great wilds of the
West there is a mountain named Ao-ao-chu, where the sun and
the moon set. There is an animal here with heads on the right
and left named P'ing-p'eng. There is Shaman Mountain. There
is Valley Mountain. There is Golden Gate Mountain and a person named Huang-chi's Corpse. There are single-winged birds
who fly in pairs. There is a white bird with green wings, yellow
tail, and a black beak. There is a red dog called Celestial Dog.
Wherever he descends, war occurs. South of the Western Sea
at the edge of the shifting sands beyond the Red River and before the Black River is a great mountain called K'un-lun."

Mount Kunlun had three levels: the lowest, "Cool Breeze,"
the middle, "Hanging Garden," and the topmost, "Upper
Heaven." The top level was associated with the activity of *wu*
shamans who performed rain dances, brought down ancestral
spirits and the souls of the dead, pacified the earth, and invited
spirits to important rituals. Kunlun was the cosmic pillar con-
necting heaven, earth, and hell, through which the shamans
passed on their way to other worlds to communicate with the
dead.

Bumping along, I asked my own questions of heaven: Are
mountains really mountains? Are mountains a form of enlightenment? Are rivers mountains running? Can we walk through
them? Why do mountains walk through us?

The paintings in the New York exhibition that took my fancy
were three leaves from an album of twelve by the Ming Dynasty
painter Song Xu, who lived alone as an untonsured monk behind a Taoist temple. The mountains were painted with pale

Leaf C, *Mt. Tai*

ink; they were smoke on silk the color of cinnamon, elegant in their remoteness and stark in their tranquillity.

To make a painting of a mountain was to engage in meditation in action. The *chi* of the mountain entered the heart of the painter. Its unbound energy moved ink and brush, but the artist first had to understand the mountain, to have swallowed it whole. To view the finished scroll of a sacred mountain was

Leaf E, *Shaoshi*

thought to be the same as traveling there: it represented spiritual progress and altered the life of the viewer, just as walking up its steep slopes changed the consciousness of the pilgrim making the ascent.

The first of the three leaves was *Mount Tai*. The whole mountain is shown, its rough slopes poured and piled up to a towering summit lined with pines. Clouds flowed down around the

Leaf F, *Tianti*

base, becoming milk rivers, and here and there tiny monastery buildings provided vantage points on this cosmic pillar as one ascended to heaven. There was always a human presence on these mountains. Even the pavilion at the top of Mount Tai was canopied by pines, as if to show that on the topknot of sacred mysteries, a pilgrim might feel at home.

Shaoshi depicted a cave on the side of Mount Song that can be found behind the Shaolin monastery. Set in the middle of a square mass of rock with vertical walls and a flat top, the interior of the cave was illuminated, and seated within was Bodhidharma, the Indian monk who brought Chan (Zen) Buddhism to China in 520 A.D.

Leaf F of the album, *Tianti*, which means "heavenly stairs," was a view of the steps that often ascended sacred mountains and the endurance it took to get to the top. Three-quarters of the way up, a lone pilgrim rested beneath a wind-bent pine tree, overlooking a sheer drop into an abyss. Far below, a worker with a bamboo broom swept away all traces of the pilgrim's footsteps, as if he had not passed by at all.

We crossed the Min River three times. Meltwater from the high mountains had not yet come down, and young couples dug river gravel, carrying it home in baskets. Old men with bamboo fishing poles waded out from the shallows into deeper water, where raw sewage poured in, to catch their evening meal. The river flowed from peaks at the northeastern edge of the Tibetan plateau behind us and I kept craning my head, trying to make out Emei Shan, but pollution continued to refashion the world as a flat place. Maybe there was no mountain to climb; maybe the mountain was climbing me.

The new sign over the entrance to Emei Shan town read: "Most beautiful mountain in the world." It was part of the Chinese government's program of rebuilding and demoting Buddhist sacred sites into tourist spots. In this state Buddhism, tickets for entry are sold.

Until the Cultural Revolution in 1966, the Chinese Communist Party granted religious freedom to Buddhists despite a Marxist antagonism toward religion, but there were strings attached. This precious freedom was only for those whose political attitudes were "progressive" or correct by Mao's ever changing standards. In 1949 Buddhist monks were executed for being landlords and monasteries were burned as houses of superstition. Buddhist practice continued, nevertheless, waxing and waning with the political winds. In 1956, 37,000 people visited Emei Shan, and the other "famous mountains" were visited on special holidays such as New Year's or the Buddha's birthday.

Mao had a nostalgic connection to Buddhism that dated back to his provincial childhood in Hunan. When he was a boy his mother often visited a Buddhist shrine to pray for his health, then burned incense and made Mao eat the ashes. When the Chairman visited his village in the 1950s during the Great Leap Forward he found that the shrine had been dismantled only weeks before, the bricks used in a backyard furnace for making steel. The sight saddened him: "It should have been left alone. Without money to see the doctors, poor farmers could still come and pray to the gods and eat the incense ashes (as I did). The shrine could lift their spirits, give them hope. People need this kind of help and encouragement."

But Mao's nostalgia failed to prevent what became Buddhism's and Taoism's slow and painful decimation by the Party. By the end of the Cultural Revolution there were no temples and monasteries, no monks, abbots, regents, or lamas, no *sangha*, or Buddhist community, left.

We spent the night at a hotel catering to Chinese tourists going up the mountain. My translator, Zha Yu, who preferred her adopted American name of Vivian, was young and efficient, bright and well traveled. The daughter of a physicist, she had been allowed to travel out of the country, had seen the Louvre, and knew which films were being censored in China. Her regular job at a Chengdu television studio was not so busy that she couldn't moonlight as a translator. She had read the poems of

Meng Chiao, Li Ho, Su T'ung Po, and Tu Fu, and knew a little about Buddhism, though she thought it odd that I wanted to climb all the way up a sacred mountain when I could have been driven.

The Chinese phrase for "going on a pilgrimage," *ch'ao-shan chin-hsiang*, actually means "paying one's respects to the mountain," as if the mountain were an empress or an ancestor before whom one must kneel. In China, sacred travel and the cult of the mountain were endemic. The recorded history of Taoism began during the second century A.D., and regarded mountains as home to immortals and as places where magic herbs to aid transcendence could be found. Confucians saw mountains as emblems of world order. In the Chou Dynasty beginning in 1027 B.C., imperial altars were built where emperors came to pray for prosperity. Heaven, earth, and man—the three mainstays of Chinese cosmology—were linked by the country's vertiginous peaks.

The meaning of pilgrimage changed when Taoists set up their mountain altars and Buddhist monks began plying the trails. For them pilgrimage was not only paying homage to a place of power, but also the transformation of the inner and outer environment through the physical act of walking, every step and breath altering the atmosphere, path and goal becoming the same. I thought of Mao's Long March, how step by step, year by year, his humanitarian ideals and visions of Marxist liberation were ground down to ego and tyranny.

In the evening we walked to the foot of the mountain. The main street of Emei Shan town unrolled in a single line to its base. The air was balmy and young couples walked hand in hand from shop to shop, then to a small pavilion at the top of the street where the stores stopped and the mountain began. In ancient times the name *Chu* alluded not only to the region now called Sichuan, but also to the mountain, Emei Shan. Also called Lofty Eyebrows Mountain, it is traditionally thought to be the abode of the bodhisattva of pervading goodness, the protector of all those who teach the Dharma, the one who is the embodiment of essential sameness, the unifying thread that strings together all disparate things.

Across a narrow irrigation ditch that followed the road, a young, dark-faced farmer had just finished plowing his rice field. As he unharnessed his water ox, I asked if I could watch. He smiled proudly. "This is not my field or my ox but I farm it for the owners and get half the value of the crop." Forty years earlier over 25 million landlords were executed by Mao's army in an effort to purge the country of just these kinds of relationships.

I touched the neck of the ox. The wooden yoke, arched in the middle where it rested on the animal's neck, was shaped like the arched gate at the entrance to the farmstead. The farmer bade us good night and led the ox down a narrow path toward a shed.

As light left the sky, the moon rose shining in each of the flooded fields as if they were bowls and the plowed earth a roiling sea of black. Overhead a white cloud dissected trees. Was this the white milk road of early landscape paintings that led up the mountain to heaven?

"The road to Chu is hard and steep, steep as climbing to the sky!" That's what the poet Li Po once wrote. Li Po was born in Sichuan Province and honored Emei Shan as a perfect mountain that could turn him into an immortal. He probably climbed Emei Shan or at least gazed at it from afar. He also wrote, "In the West at Mount Taibo, there is a bird road that can cut across the summit of Mount Emei."

In the morning, after a breakfast of congee (a rice gruel), instant coffee, white bread, and jam, Mr. Tong drove us to the base of the mountain. The day before, when the plane had descended through clouds and smog, I knew I was dropping into a beautiful country that had been made into a living hell. Nations can be shattered, cultures can be laid on history's anvil, twisted, flattened, and decimated, but a mountain remains a mountain. Now I had to rise out of that hell on foot and I knew it would be hard.

Mr. Tong waved good-bye and said he would return in four days. Tourist buses filled the parking lot as he wove down the hill. Hefting our rucksacks onto our backs, we turned to face our pilgrim's task. Despite the stairs that were so small we had to wrench our feet sideways, it felt good to be on our way.

Shan: mountain. *Mingshan*: sacred mountain. All pilgrims stepped onto a path. The path led to a mountain. The way was crowded. From rows of rickety tables, vendors sold herbs picked on Emei Shan's slopes—ginseng, fungi, and a bundle of golden plant hairs given the shape of a dog; also amulets, walking sticks, maps, and cold spring water. Medicinal herbs seem to grow more profusely on holy mountains. No one knows why.

At a little over 6,000 feet the air was thick and humid. Women passed with baskets of strawberries and young men slung fresh-picked vegetables on their backs. Crowds of golden monkeys gathered, demanding and taking peanuts from the hands of Buddhist pilgrims and Chinese tourists. Further up the mountain an old man stepped out on the path behind me, bamboo broom in his hand, a thin long pipe in his mouth, and as I walked by, he hawked, spit, then swept my tracks clean. Trackless, I continued on.

Shu dao nan: The road to Shu is hard. There is no top, no goal. Only this hard path made of stones, the dry instruction of climbing a mountain. Every step up is a movement away from the realm of human sorrows, from the Middle Kingdom teetering between heaven and hell, from all suffering. Every step down is a slide back into it, until up and down become the same thing.

Up and up we continued, each sideways, cramped step a reminder of how difficult it is to relinquish habitual thought. "Abandon hope all ye who enter here." Dante's words had been posted above the door of the meditation hall where I sat for three and a half months in 1978. They might have said: "Welcome to the heaven or hell of your own making. Good luck climbing out." This I had already learned: If you weed the garden of your mind properly, there will be no hope and no fear, just the hard vigor of life as it plays itself out in you. But the body still resists and the mind curvets like a missile shot off and gone wild.

Emei Shan was arduous in a senseless way. I had some questions for heaven and I asked them: Why steps on a mountain path? Who carried these stones? There were stairs on the three other sacred Buddhist mountains and on the five imperial mountains and they were well used: a seventeenth-century record showed that six hundred thousand pilgrims had climbed Mount Tai. Does climbing a mountain teach about transforming effort to effortlessness? Are the two really the same, or was I a fool, were we all fools to do these things? Poor fool that I am, and often grinning through streams of sweat, I clambered on.

Every sacred mountain has its founding story. A monk or layman has a vision of a certain site and of the bodhisattva who inhabits the place. I don't know what atlas guides him, points his feet, or how he knows where to scuffle away the dirt and uncover the thin spot, the umbilicus of the mountain where its divinity is finally exposed, but it happens.

Emei Shan was opened by a man named Pu Gong. One day he was gathering some herbs on the mountain and began following deer tracks. These led him to the top of the mountain, then disappeared. Suddenly Pu Gong heard music. When he looked up he saw humans, some on horseback, drifting toward the summit on clouds. But one figure was riding a six-tusked albino elephant and above his head glowed a halo of colored light. Pu Gong was so moved by this vision that he took off and walked all the way to India—a journey that took three months—and visited a Buddhist monk to tell him his tale. The monk listened, nodded, then passed the story on to his teacher, who interpreted Pu Gong's tale as the coming of the Bodhisattva Samantabhadra to the mountain. Pu Gong was instructed to return to Emei Shan and build a temple. Called "First Audience Hall," it was burned down by Mao's Red Guard and has since been reconstructed.

In the first century, the poet Fan Zhen wrote this quatrain:

"We move to Mount Emei's highest peak;
Who knows how many thousands of layers of crags
    and cliffs?
A mountain monk smiles as he tells the story of
    Master Pu:
It was here that the white deer once left its tracks."

The further up we went, the fewer people we saw. The climate felt tropical, not alpine; I was bathed in sweat and the skies revealed nothing, no glimpses of high peaks. Vivian said she was too young to know much of what went on during Liberation—except that her physicist father and artist mother were put in labor reform camps where they were "struggled against." How ironic that the word *liberation* used by Mao was the same word used by American Buddhists to mean deliverance from *samsara*—human suffering—through practice. Once, going to these mountains was sanctuary, a distant retreat, a nostalgic home, a land where immortals picked herbs to prolong life, where hopping shamanic dances were danced and questions of heaven were posed. I wondered if, after the tyrannies of Mao and the Cultural Revolution, a culture could come back into being, if the human spirit could be stirred? When I asked Vivian, she said she was too young to know what had been lost and didn't see that there was a problem.

Sweating and listless, I began coughing. Having come from Hong Kong with a cold, my chest had tightened. This wasn't even a mountain by Tibetan standards, only the foothills of the Himalayas. I had walked in many mountains but nothing resembled Emei Shan: so many stairs, so many people. It was hard to see where I was, to frame the scape. Was this the axis mundi from which the spirit soared? Were the stairs the rungs of the metaphorical ladder on which shamans climbed and the mind scratched a hole to see through?

Hogars, the young men who carried people up the mountain on narrow, slung-seated palanquins, hounded us. "Please let us carry you," they beseeched. "Bu, bu, bu, bu." No thanks, I said, and told Vivian I was shocked at the idea. "But humans carrying humans has had a long history in China," Vivian exclaimed. "It's perfectly natural."

Tea shops, temples, pavilions, and pagodas dotted the mountain. We stopped often to rest and drink cool Emei Shan spring water. At Elegant Sound Pavilion, a tumbling cataract sounded like rolling thunder. Ox Heart Pavilion was flanked on either side by the stream, which was split again by Ox Heart Rock. Golden frogs croaked and the shade of ancient nanmu trees cooled us. A Ming dynasty monk, Hong Ji, planted 69,707 of these trees, chanting a sutra and prostrating after each one went into the ground. In this way, he kept count. With only a few remaining, their shade in hot Sichuan sun still soothes tired pilgrims.

I stepped and counted. One stair equalled one of Hong Ji's trees. Rounding a bend, I entered the cool breeze of a narrow ravine called "A Strip of Heaven Cleavage." Did the rhododendrons that flowered on those steep cliffs have to climb the stairs to flower there?

Every step seemed to provoke in me more speculation. But the Chinese are still afraid to give the wrong answer. We passed a skinny porter sound asleep on his palanquin by the side of the path. A friend who had climbed Emei Shan in 1984 said the hogars had passed her on the mountain carrying a dead woman. They had wrapped her up and laid her on the sling as if she were sleeping. When my friend asked if the woman was dead the hogars said, "She's not dead, she's just very, very tired."

I asked Vivian about the mountain's geology. Was it wind or glaciers that carved these cliffs? "The gods cut through the mountains with their swords," she replied laughing. "That's the story Chinese people love to tell. Of course, I don't believe in such things."

We crossed Myriad Years Bridge, built in the Chin dynasty (265–420 A.D.). All around were flowers, ferns, trees, and bamboo. Here, the crowds of pilgrims began to thin out and the monkeys became more agressive. An old woman from a tea shop threatened the monkeys with a stick, clearing the path for us to proceed. Up more steps, they screeched at us menacingly from tree branches. Vivian pressed close to me, confessing that she was scared.

Tired, out of breath, and thirsty, we stopped at a tea shop for a cool drink. It was an open-air hut with a thatched roof perched on a precipitous ledge of rock. A side of pork hanging from a hook and covered with flies swung in the breeze. On the wall a large poster of Christ loomed, blood rolling down his arms and legs from stigmata. "We are Catholics," the two women who ran the place said proudly. "On a Buddhist mountain?" I asked. They shrugged. "We can make money here," they replied.

As I rested my feet and looked out across the green chasm toward India, I thought of the first time I saw my teacher, an incarnate Tibetan lama. He was riding across a field on a white horse. I asked him why he had chosen a white horse and he said, "This is like the white horse who carried the teachings to the west." Then he galloped away, laughing.

We started up again. Six women passed us going down the other way. I expected them to be tourists, but these were Buddhist pilgrims singing a Buddhist song. They stopped and blessed us: "Buddha's breath blows on you," and kept walking.

Buddhism was introduced in China during the reign of the Han emperor, Ming-ti, during the years 58 to 75 A.D. He had come to power after the delusional reign of Wang Mang, who enacted the rituals of the mythical Chou dynasty, wearing costumes made especially for the occasion. His real-life agrarian reform was disastrous: he made all land the property of the state with the profits from a central field going to the throne. A peasant revolt resulted. When their army took over the imperial palace, they found Wang wearing his costume and praying. They beheaded him.

The emperor Ming-ti suceeded Wang Mang. He restored the caravan routes to the west—to India, Persia, and the Roman Empire—and in doing so, opened the way for Buddhist teachings to travel the northern and southern Silk Roads from India into China. There was not just one Silk Road, but many that traversed Himalayan mountains and rolled across 17,000-foot-high plateaus and parched deserts from oasis to oasis. On these, scrolls of sutras were packed alongside imported glass-ware and incense on the backs of donkeys and camels and dis-seminated into Asia.

Ming-ti had become interested in Buddhism after dreaming of a gold statue representing the Buddha. He sent officials to India to investigate the teachings of the Gautama. Months later the emissaries returned in the company of two Indian monks who led a white horse carrying sacred scrolls, the Bud-dha's teachings.

Buddhism first gained a foothold in China's "barbaric" north. A scholar-monk, Fo-t'u-teng, was on his way to the city of Lo-yang to translate sutras, but on arrival he found the city had been burned and overtaken by Mongolians. Cleverly, Fo-t'u-teng sought an audience with the new leader. As the leader looked on, the monk filled his begging bowl with water and said a prayer; a lotus flower blossomed. Impressed by the magic, though ignorant of real Buddhist teachings, Lo became a pa-tron of the Dharma. Buddhism flourished because it fused with Taoism and local folk religions rather than obliterating them.

Later, in the early Tang, a monk named Xuanzang walked to Kashmir and Nalanda via Gansu and the high passes of Af-ghanistan, stayed sixteen years, and returned over those same high pastures of the Pamirs with 527 boxes of Buddhist scrip-tures. Accompanied by a mythical monkey king, Xuanzang be-came the subject of the Ming dynasty novel *Journey to the West*, and helped popularize Buddhist teachings about self-delusion and desire, impermanence, and suffering.

"The most important state is to be without desire," read the sign above the Age-Old Trees Monastery. "If you are without desire you have a real treasure." We entered a courtyard through an imposing gate where a monk sold us tickets out of a plastic bag, a practice imposed by the government. Saffron robes hung in the sun to dry from second-story balconies. An old monk sashayed by with the balanced, free-gaited walk of a practitioner. I asked if I could speak with him. He shook his head no, then disappeared around the back. "He came from Shaolin Monastery and he's been here for forty years. He's a master of the martial arts," a young monk informed me.

During the Cultural Revolution, many Buddhist and Taoist temples and monasteries were burned down, defaced, or hacked to pieces. Now the Chinese government had begun rebuilding them as tourist sites where, almost incidentally, Buddhism could once again be practiced. But what kind of practice takes place under these conditions? Were these "tourist monks" only?

Too late for lunch, we bought cookies and sodas at the monastery's store. Vivian grabbed the package of biscuits to check the date on the back. "These are two years old!" she shrieked, throwing them back at the monk who had sold them to us, chastizing him for being rude. He looked at her bewildered.

At the next stop we came on sixty Buddhist pilgrims sitting by the side of the trail and rested with them for a while. They were mostly old women, eager to talk. One of them massaged my head and back because she saw that I was unwell. My cold had turned to bronchitis. When I asked if they had been to Emei Shan often, they all said they had, before the Cultural Revolution, and since Deng came to power they were allowed to make their once-yearly pilgrimage. Relaxing in the sun, I inquired about their practice. One woman said, "We have all suffered so much. We have had many hardships and so we pray for peace and health, and hope that maybe the Buddha will give our children more than we have had."

At the next tea shop up the mountain, we ordered lunch. A wind-torn poster nailed to the wall showed Greek islands floating in azure water. A side of pork was brought down and slabs were cut from it; vegetables were stir-fried in a wok over a coal fire nested in a tile basin. When Vivian expressed her fear of the monkeys, a young man at the tea shop, a nephew of the owners, offered to accompany us up the mountain. He said the monkeys farther up were more dangerous and on hearing that, Vivian began the bargaining.

Incongruously dressed for the mountains, the young man wore trousers, a blue V-neck sweater, a sport jacket, and beige hard-soled shoes. A price for his services was agreed upon and he took down his hand-carved walking stick from the wall. "He'll protect you," the women shouted to us as we started up the mountain. Although he dressed like a city kid, we found out that he had been born on Emei Shan, had never been to school because there are none in this part of the province, and couldn't read. With a wife and child to support, he worked as a mountain guide.

A few miles up the path the monkeys began to appear. They leaped out in front of us searching our hands and grabbing at our bags for peanuts. Moments before, a monkey had torn the earrings from a young woman's ears—we had heard her screaming. Our guide chased them away with his walking stick.

The trail suddenly steepened. "This is the Jiu Shi Dao Guai," our young leader announced. It meant "Ninety-Nine Hairpin Bends." He strode effortlessly ahead in his city-slicker shoes, nodding hello to a couple hauling onions and cabbages in two baskets suspended on a long shoulder pole. Two miles worth of cut stone steps later, we arrived at Nine Ancient Caverns, a cave carved by water in limestone. Slippery from bat guano, the stairs descended into the dark. The bats were so thick they hit the backs of our heads. In China, bats—*qiubang*—symbolize good luck.

Ju-shan: to enter. To step inside a mountain through a cave, called a *dongtian*, meant gaining access to its chthonic power. It was to enter the realm of the sacred; to mix with the mountain's guest list of immortals called *xian*: odd beings with human bodies and dragon faces, or two heads, or a monkey's body with a human face, or a headless torso that is also a face.

At the bottom of a long flight of steps, we came into a room. Candles were lit around a grotesque, potbellied, laughing god riding a tiger. This was the postmodern Chinese version of Maitreya, the future Buddha, but a sign simplified it to: "The god of wealth." A tin can was provided for contributions (undoubtedly by the Chinese government working through the monastery). "The god of greed" might have been a more apt name. Had we come all this way to throw yuan into a tin can and pray for money?

I was desperate to get out of there. Running back up the steps, I slipped in bat dung and screamed. Finally emerging, I took a deep breath and inhaled pine wind and evening air.

Why climb a mountain? Outside, purple and white rhododendrons erupted in flower. A monkey leaped from a tree and ripped the pocket off my coat looking for peanuts. A cuckoo cuckooed. The old man in blue pantaloons who had swept my human tracks with his broom had not swept the monkey's. Perhaps, as the poet Nanao Sakaki wrote, there was no climbing going on, only something moving up and down in the air.

Contained in China's earliest records are the words of emperors, Taoists, Buddhists, Confucians, painters, and poets who made pilgrimages to these peaks, praying for prosperity, searching for immortality, seeking sanctuary: mountain as refuge, mountain as home.

Charles Hartman, a scholar of Chinese religion, wrote: "The universe is a mountain whose summit is spiritual perfection; who ascends the mountain attains that perfection; and his body unites with the perfection of the summit and becomes one with the universe. The spiritual life is thus a journey to the summit of the mountain."

In eighth-century China, a meticulous scholasticism gave way to spiritual transformation through practice. Chan (Zen) Buddhists walked the mountains and valleys, their perambulations representing the inward movement toward one's original nature. Mahayana and Vajrayana Buddhists came to regard the physical world as *dharmakaya*, in which the body of the Buddha was one and the same as the mountain or the terrestial world. Physical and holy merged. Walking up a mountain was also a way of traversing the thirty-two distinctive marks of the Buddha's body. For example, monasteries were placed on sites that resembled his topknotted head, and on his flat tongue were valleys where livestock were grazed.

Taoist priests officiated at an altar called Tung-an. It was a table that represented a sacred mountain, divided into eight squares corresponding to compass points, with the central space being the axis mundi. During the ceremony, the priest ascended the metaphorical mountain to the golden summit where he arrived at the source of all things, the Tao.

The Buddhist-Taoist mountain was both macro and micro: a picture of the universe as body; a representation of body as sacred mountain. To walk on the mountain was also to move inside the mountain where earth was aerated by *chi*. Through such intimate knowledge of the place, the priest attained a spiritual body; he danced a dance called *yu pu* in which he traced his steps along the stars of the Big Dipper to the central pole star.

We stopped to buy more plastic bottles of Emei Shan water and to give away the peanuts we'd bought at the bottom because it was too dangerous to carry them—the monkeys might snatch our backpacks and carry them away. Unlacing my boots for a moment to cool my feet, I had more questions of heaven: Was the mountain real or metaphorical? Was it cosmos or a pile of dirt and rock to make up a single peak? Was it a human body or a metaphysical corpus? Was the "I" the same as the "one" of the mountain? Would ascent confer *samadhi*?

Two more hours of trudging, and the mountain opened up into a great scarp, a curtain of rock like an amphitheater, down which a shoestring waterfall dribbled. A narrow trail traversed the bottom of the headwall. I had to tilt my head all the way back to see the top. Then the rock blackened with rain.

"Heaven rains water down and earth's *chi* pushes upward." That, from an old text. Night fell. Up ahead, on a far ridge, I could see lights—a tiny cluster of buildings. "That's where we will spend the night," Vivian told me.

It was utterly dark when we walked into the White Cloud Monastery perched on a thin promontory of rock. We bought our tickets inside the humble meditation hall, a room the size of a two-horse barn with a crude statue of the Buddha on a dirty altar. Vivian and I performed the usual three prostrations while a young monk in tennis shoes with a criminal's scarred face rang the gong. Then we asked if they would make us dinner.

The kitchen was black with grime. A chalkboard menu hung

on the wall. Vivian ordered, but it didn't seem to matter. The cook made whatever he liked. The first platter of food was a charred black lump—meat or fish? Ever vigilant, Vivian asked. The monks shrugged. Grasshoppers, maybe, then laughter. Plates of vegetables swimming in rancid oil were passed. I drank tea, ate rice, fished for something edible. "Is the cook a monk?" I asked. No, he was hired from the valley. The monks stood in a tight circle around us with folded arms, hawking, and spitting, and staring.

After the meal, we were shown to our rooms: they were frigid, dirty, and rat infested, with cobwebs swinging across the rafters. A monk deposited an armload of quilts on the bed and a small pillow covered with a dirty orange towel. I heard laughter. Vivian and the other monks were in the sitting room watching television, a love story made in Taiwan, so I joined them.

We asked the men why they had become monks. There was a silence. Then one said it was because he was in trouble. Another said it was better than anything else he could find. Like our guide, he'd been born in the mountains where there are no schools and he still couldn't read or write. But life was easy here. I asked if there was an abbot or a teacher with whom they studied the Dharma. No. There were seven districts on the mountain and this monastery was controlled by the one at Elephant Washing Pool. How did they learn to be monks, then? I asked. They said that sometimes they listened to tapes of talks by teachers from the city. They were only allowed to leave the monastery once a year to go home to visit their parents and families. Otherwise, they never left the mountain.

It's said that when Buddhism came to China it degenerated into ancestor worship, but as in all countries the profundity of the practice varies. I had read about a Chinese monk practicing Chan, who described his meditation experience as *p'iao-p'iao mang-mang-ti,* which means "floating sublimely." When I asked these monks about their practice, they hesitated. Then the old one who had not spoken said, "We chant twice a day. Then we watch television." He bent down to put on his sandals. "The most important thing is to remain without desire, especially toward women," he said, averting his eyes from Vivian, as if his only teaching had come from the sign above the monastery a few miles below.

When the TV show came to a finale, they turned the set off. I wondered on whose back it had been carried up the mountain. One young man said, "We are a poor monastery. There are only three monks here. The others come up from the valley. In fact there are more monkeys on this mountain than monks," he said, laughing.

Too cold to sleep, too cold to wake, I hung on some edge, the entry to the abyss where one flings oneself to shave away ego. There was such a place on this mountain, where you could look off a sheer edge all the way down the seven-story mountain. The walls of the small monastery room were ice and the cobwebs swung against my shoulder, falling onto my face. A gong rang for no apparent reason. I understood then that there is no sacred mountain and no secular mountain. All are holy, all are ordinary, just rock paths, struggling trees, flying springs, dirty monasteries, melting snow. To think of a place as sacred, what did it mean? In sleep, the shadow of the mountain lay across a dry plain and out of those shadows, came what? You cannot walk a mountain with expectations or you will not see where you are, and the mountain will not see you.

The shadow lifted. Another gong sounded. It was 4:00 A.M., time for morning practice.

A Tibetan lama, Thubten Jigme Norbu, said, "A mountain stands as an example of something immutable. No one can take it away. A flood cannot take it; a fire cannot destroy it. This inner mountain stands for our spiritual growth. Too often we don't make a spiritual mountain but build up pride and jealousy, mountains of anger. And our minds move so fast."

The next morning we began the last walk to the top. Hens pecked crumbs from the dirt floor of a tea shop, its mud and wattle walls graced by posters of Western-style motels with sumptuous interiors. At almost 10,000 feet we skirted snow on the trail; the men and women who lived and worked at that altitude were ruddy faced. Snarled, mossy trees lined the path, which opened onto an abyss. I stepped to the edge and peered straight down past vertical limestone karsts into a bottomless pit of green. There were no guardrails: this was the place where both ritual and actual suicides had taken place for thousands of years. I imagined myself falling. Who doesn't desire extinguishment? Nirvana means, literally, "a blowing out." The ground was wet and I wondered if the cliff would hold. Perhaps this was the only way to see the mountain, by jumping down its flank and into its belly.

We walked on, past another pavilion, a tea shop, and a temple where three monks throwing Frisbees looked over a young German woman traveling alone and leaped for joy when she bought a ticket to spend the night there. Just below the Golden Summit, Vivian insisted that we take the tourists' cable car to the top instead of walking the pilgrim's stairs. There was no dissuading her. After a cold wait on a bare cement terrace, we crowded into the tram and swung up an almost vertical incline.

On the day called I-wei which is July 24, 1177, the poet Fan Ch'eng-ta took three days to make the ascent of Emei Shan and wrote this account:

I returned to the chapel on the cliff to offer up a prayer. Soon, a dense mist arose on all sides, blending everything into a single whiteness. A monk said, 'This is the Silvery World.' After a while, a heavy rain fell and the mist dispersed. The monk said, 'This is the Rain that Cleanses the Cliff. Buddha's Halo is about to appear.' Flossy clouds once again spread out below the cliff, billowing upward until they reached only several tens of feet below the top. The clouds smoothed themselves out like a floor of jade. There was a sudden rain and droplets flew about. I looked down at the middle of the cliff—there was a large halo lying on top of the smooth clouds. Encircling it were three rings, each containing blue, yellow, red, and green colors. The center of the halo was empty, bright, dense, and clear. Each observer could see his form appear in the empty bright area without the slightest degree of obscurity, just like a mirror. When one raised one's hands and moved one's legs, the reflection indicated this without showing anyone else's form. The monk said, 'This is the Halo that Captures the Body.' When this halo vanished, winds arose from the mountains in front and the clouds quickly drifted away.

The tram door opened onto the Golden Summit of Emei Shan. I stepped out and turned slowly in place. The peak had been bulldozed into a large paved square thronged by Chinese tourists wearing ankle-length green army coats, and from some unknown source Strauss waltzes blasted across the top of the mountain. The coats, all exactly the same, had been rented from vendors near the tram station. Beyond was a parking lot; a road had been built up the back of the mountain so that tourists could be driven to the top instead of walking the pilgrims' route. A photographer with a box camera took souvenir snapshots, his pet monkey tied by a leash to the tripod. Shops and small restaurants ringed the square and behind them stood three cheesy, would-be Las Vegas–style hotels, partly constructed. Then I saw the source of the music: a radio station with huge outdoor speakers wedged between the hotels and a karaoke hall fronted by fake Greek columns.

Stone steps led to the topknot of the summit. A young woman in red patent leather high heels sat on a chair and slurped noodles while her boyfriend sold tickets to the summit's one remaining temple. At least there was this remnant of Buddhism. The wind howled, and after the tropical heat in which we had climbed I felt chilled. The temple was tiny, its paint peeling. I walked all the way around its perimeter, then discovered that its doors were locked. Out in front, an old woman had stuck a burning joss stick, big as a firecracker, into a large bronze incense brazier. She had buried her head in her hands and was sobbing.

On the far side of the temple, at the very edge of the cliff, a guardrail held back throngs of Chinese tourists waiting for "Buddha's Halo," the spectral event that Fan Ch'eng-ta had seen at sundown eight hundred years earlier. But this day clouds obscured the view. Finally the disgruntled crowd dispersed as it grew dark, returning to their gaudy, unheated hotels. We followed.

Behind the desk two young men—thugs in dark glasses— sullenly gave us our keys. The beds in my room had gold spreads with ruffles. It was, after all, the Golden Summit. The radio station's outdoor speakers switched from Strauss to Chinese pop music and tourists in army greatcoats strode around the central square as if doing maneuvers. Out back in the courtyard of a small monastery, two monks played badminton in frozen dirt next to a microwave transmitter that had been planted in their midst as if it were a sacred tree.

I fished a poem by Yeats from my pocket, the one the monkey had not torn. It was about the mythical sacred mountain of India, Meru, and it began:

> Civilisation is hooped together, brought
> Under a rule, under the semblance of peace
> By manifold illusion; but man's life is thought,
> And he, despite his terror, cannot cease
> Ravening through century after century,
> Ravening, raging, and uprooting that he may come
> Into the desolation of reality. . . .

The room was dark and cold. In the gloom, I pulled the gold spread from the bed and wrapped it around my shoulders. China was experiencing a time of peace, but life here felt illusory. It was a dictated peace, one that could be torn away at a moment's notice.

When a ceiling of clouds dropped to the ground, the monks went inside and the white badminton net trembled in a sudden wind, catching, then dropping the last light. If human life is only thought, if we create and destroy for no reason, if all sacredness is only human perception, the need to believe just another projection by which we locate ourselves, then why climb a mountain, why does a mountain climb me?

My cold worsened. When Vivian knocked on the door to call me for dinner, I had already begun crying and couldn't stop. True, I was cold and sick, but it was more than that. When Vivian asked what was wrong, all I could think of to say was, "Nobody cares. Nobody is indignant about what has happened here." Which probably wasn't completely accurate, but true enough.

The hotel's dining room was in the basement—colder, more dank and dirty than the rest of the hotel. It was hard to eat because my hands were shaking. I was taking a short journey to a country with a long history and nothing seemed true. Vivian, trying earnestly to be cheerful, promised we would see the Buddha's Halo at dawn, as if my disappointment at missing it that afternoon was the cause of my tears. How could I explain that I had not climbed Emei Shan for spiritual souvenirs. It didn't matter. I nodded obediently: Yes, I'd be ready at dawn.

Later, in bed, my chest tightened and it hurt to breathe. I knew enough medicine to know the pain was pulmonary, not cardiac, and as I drifted to sleep my crying jag came to an end. I recalled the night my Tibetan teacher arrived two hours late to give a talk and upon surveying the roomful of overeager students, said, "Please, go home to your depressions." Then he left.

I tried to visualize the mountain beneath me. Which questions of heaven should I ask of it? A mountain is a whole world and spirit is a flea that jumps ship from one hot-bodied infinity to another. That's about all I knew that night. Also, everything I could say about myself at that moment could be attributed to the mountain or vice versa: its abysses, its formlessness, its flat places, its milk and roughness, its fevered sweat, its delusions, its waters and scents.

In the morning the light on Emei Shan was the color of cinnamon. I thought of the three album leaves of sacred mountains I'd seen at the Met. They showed the mountain as sanctuary, its summit looming gold above a floating sea of clouds. Leaf E revealed the illumined interior of the *dongtian*—the cave—where one enters into the circulating power of the mountain.

Leaf F gave a view of the steps to the top, the arduous ascent, and the old man with the broom, like a figure of death, sweeping my footprints away.

After sunrise the speakers began blaring karaoke music and the photographer with the monkey set up his box camera in the frigid square. A man in a green army coat emerged from a shop with a steaming jar of mountain tea. He spit at the monkey's feet, gave a cursory glance in the direction of the small temple at the top, still locked, then climbed aboard a waiting bus. Like the Great Wall, a curtain of pollution finally swallowed him from sight. It was May 8, the Buddha's birthday.

Shu dao nan: The road to Shu is hard. It is like climbing to the stars. There are many false summits along the way and at the top, there is only emptiness. The beginning and the end are the same.

From

Tian Wen

or

Questions

of Heaven

15

Setting out from the Gulf of Brightness and going to rest in
the Vale of Murk, from the dawn until the time of darkness,
how many miles is the journey?

81

When Ping summons up the rain, how does he raise it? When
those different parts were assembled and joined on to a deer,
how were they fitted into shape?

73

On that westward journey from Zu to Qiong-shi how did Yi
cross the heights? And when Gun turned into a brown bear,
how did the shamans bring him back to life?

羅峰晴雲
己未年夏武戟月藝兒

DISPOSABLE

PANDAS

The ultimate responsibility for saving the panda in its
natural home rests with China: it alone can implement
the measures needed for the animal's protection. The rest
of the world must, however, offer guidance, funds, and
moral support. The gravity of the situation represents
both hope and opportunity. But if we fail to make the
correct choices now, the last pandas will disappear, leaving us with the nostalgia of a failed epic, an indictment of
civilization as destroyer. We cannot recover a lost world.

—George Schaller, *The Last Panda*

This morning I watched a water ox bathe in a small river. He
had wandered away from the others who were being yoked and
slid down a muddy bank to wallow in cool water. It was an un-
usual sight in China: an animal at its own leisure, enjoying life.
Soon enough, the farmer came for him, willow whip in hand,
and led him back into service: pulling a wooden plow across unplanted, flooded rice fields.

Mr. Tong was driving me to the Wolong Panda Preserve in
the mountains northwest of Chengdu. Though I had come to
China to climb Buddhist mountains, I also wanted to see where
and how the animals lived, if their culture had survived. Seven
hundred and twenty-five years ago, Marco Polo wrote, "On

leaving Ch'eng-tu-fu the traveler rides for five days through plain and valley, passing villages and hamlets in plenty. The people here live on the yield of the earth. The country is infested with lions, bears, and other wild beasts."

The name *Chengdu* (*Cheng-t'u*) means "official road," alluding to the distant posts where poet-scholars were once stationed while in public service. Now the narrow alleyways of its outskirts were lined with peasants called *manglie* ("blind drifters"), day laborers who had migrated to the cities between harvests to look for work. Their hoes, machetes, and hand tools were neatly rolled in bits of canvas and tucked inside threshing baskets. Their share of Deng's "glorious wealth" was a meager wage of ten to fifteen yuan a day.

When Mao walked through Chengdu on the Long March in the 1940s, he made a promise to liberate workers from dire poverty, starvation, the feudal practices of landlords, penury and unfair taxation, galvanizing the peasants into a prodigious political force. What began as a humanitarian ideal turned into government rule by brutal coercion. Utopian dreams were crushed by censoriousness and intimidation; relief from penury through land reform was given over to a collectivization of farmland so immense and thoroughgoing that the peasants were eventually stripped of everything, even something to eat. The resulting famine that gripped China from 1958 to 1961 brought about 30 million deaths. Though poverty initially had been eliminated by Mao, he grew too fond of his weapons of harassment, lawlessness, betrayal, and execution; unlike Hitler and Stalin, Mao hid while these weapons were being used.

Mao called himself *heshang dasan*—an outlaw. "I am a graduate from the University of Outlaws," he declared. *Outlaw* became a euphemism for tyrant, sycophant, and treacherous despot. He read avidly about the lives of the cruelest emperors, thinking himself to be messianic, a chosen ruler. *Heshang da-san* was an apt description. He hated state ritual and protocol, and lived and ruled beyond the law, replacing state and social conventions with customs of his own. He traveled around his country frequently, talking to local leaders face-to-face. This way, no one could know what he said to them, no one could usurp or counteract his power.

Everything he did conspired to make the political elite as well as the masses directly dependent on him and him alone. His most famous speech was called "On the Correct Handling of Contradictions among the People"—which meant being sent into exile or killed.

Original and eccentric, Mao's style was perhaps better suited to the absurdist stage of choreographer Pina Bausch than to the theatre of global politics. He was demanding, paranoid, lascivious, delusional, and impenitent. A recluse, he met foreign dignitaries in his bathrobe. He refused to wash, saying, "I bathe myself inside the bodies of women." He was an insomniac and insisted on having his personal doctor with him at all times, so that if he couldn't sleep, he had a reliable companion to chat with, usually in the middle of the night. His sexual appetite was such that he insisted on having his bed carried with him at all times for frequent sexual forays. He spent most of his days swimming and lying in bed. When times were bad, he rode around in his private railway carriage with the shades drawn down.

The Chinese people didn't know the details of Mao's private life until recently, but the lucky ones, the wily ones, did learn how to survive: by keeping a low profile; expecting betrayals from everyone and giving all their time, concern, and loyalty to the Chairman and no one else. Despite the revelations about his private life, Mao is still guardedly revered: "He had the highest ideals, but no moral backbone from which to act," a friend of mine said. "He had humble beginnings and he got lost in all his power. It was like an orchard for a starving man. Too much fruit. He ate until he was sick and then he spread that sickness everywhere."

Mao died in 1976. When Deng Xiaoping was returned to power in 1978, he declared: "To get rich is glorious." Though Deng's reforms freed the people from Mao's tyranny, there are new hardships and uncertainties. Deng's emerging "socialist market economy" and "spiritual socialism" are beset with problems. Since Tiananmen Square, people only want to make money, because money equals freedom. They aren't sure of what will happen next. For the time being, party bosses rule; corruption involving complicity between the Communist government and the Chinese mafia is common knowledge. It's the only way to get ahead. After all, China is still a dictatorship and the people have few democratic rights: no free speech, no free press, no freedom of assembly or travel, and no court of justice to represent them. "But those are Western ideas," Mr. Tong said, smiling wryly.

We passed more groups of peasants waiting by the side of the road to get hired. Of the 100 million peasants coming to cities to look for work, 40 million are unemployed. My translator said, "Sometimes bad things happen to them. They are beaten or not paid. Most people just want to make enough money to feed themselves no matter how they have to do it. Who comes into power next is a subject of great concern. If it reverts to the way it was before, while the Chairman was in power, there's going to be trouble."

But when I asked what kind of trouble, Mr. Tong and the translator shrugged. Later, someone else suggested there might be civil war between the provincial armies and rebels. "We don't need democracy; we need something like a society that is part Confucian, part Taoist, a code of conduct for the people that arises from Chinese ideals."

We stopped at a Taoist temple on the outskirts of Chengdu. Priests walked the temple grounds in gray mandarin tunics over black trousers. Their long hair was pulled up and held in place by a chopstick and cupped by a black pillbox hat with a hole for the topknot. The monks were lackluster, sour faced, and rude. One temple and courtyard gave onto another and another until, in the main hall, I stood before three statues of Lao Tzu riding a tiger, riding a cloud, and riding a crane. Slouched in a chair in a dark corner, a monk sat with his feet propped up, pressing a small radio to his ear.

Taoism and Buddhism managed to coexist happily for thousands of years, but neither had survived Mao or the daily catechism of confession and betrayal he imposed. Buddhism was silenced but, according to my friend Raoul, "Taoism got trashed." Once, Taoism had been the source of Chinese reverence for mountains and a wild spirited textbook for living. Now, the urban temples looked like tawdry museums, theme parks for the occult. Mr. Tong had wisely stayed in the car to read his book.

As we left the outer edges of Chengdu for Wolong we passed into the realm of intensive human labor: men hauling cement bridge parts, a woman pushing a bicycle with two hundred pounds of grain, humans hauling humans in rickshaws, horses pulling carts laden with lumber and bricks. Farther along, farmsteads' shaped terraces glistened with night soil and water, and phalanxes of women planted seedling rice. Here and there an apartment complex shot up on the plain, demarking what would someday be a new city. At one, stonemasons walked a shaky bamboo scaffold above the entry gate with a fanciful name taken from an American sitcom. The inner sanctum held a tipped-over statue of the "goddess of democracy"—a crude replica of the Statue of Liberty used in the 1989 Tiananmen Square demonstrations.

The film I had seen about China's bear farms was shown on British television. Filmed in Chengdu, sometimes using hidden cameras, it showed Asiatic black bears whose gallbladders had been implanted with permanant catheters. From these, bile was collected and sold as medicine. There were at least ten thousand bears kept on such farms. The bears were incarcerated in tiny cages and often kept in the courtyard of local houses or apartment buildings. A close-up showed one bear's catheter site: it was full of pus and pained the trapped bear to move at all.

Another scene showed a filthy cement pit at the bottom of a three-story building where bears were kept. For a price, the public could taunt the animals by throwing food down to them from the balconies, an urban amusement park of sorts in this all-for-profit China. I wondered if the panda, the international symbol of animal preservation, would be in better shape.

Outside the city and its sprawling, linked towns, we passed a series of big ponds. In one, an old man sat unmoving on a bamboo stool in the water, holding a fishing pole, his blue pantaloons rolled up to his knees, and a conical hat shading his face. All around him, young people were throwing nets into the water and grabbing at tiny fish. A pole-pushed sampan floated by soundlessly. On the road, a young woman wearing a white dress with lace ruffles and red high heels stepped into a bicycle rickshaw and disappeared. Near the mountains a district of sawmills lined the wide highway and government trucks carried immense logs. Could there still be virgin forests somewhere in western China? Was any habitat for the panda and other animals being preserved?

Père Armand David was a French missionary who had lived in an isolated valley in these mountains. A self-made naturalist, he recorded the first sighting of a panda in his 1875 diary: "From one year's end to another, one hears the hatchet and the axe cutting the most beautiful trees. The destruction of these primitive forests, of which there are only fragments in all of China, progresses with unfortunate speed. They will never be replaced. With the great trees will disappear a multitude of shrubs and other plants which cannot survive except in their shade; also all the animals, small and large, which need the forest in order to live and perpetuate their species."

Mr. Tong headed north and west up a narrow river valley where Teddy Roosevelt and his brother Kermit had come to shoot big game in the late 1800s. Not long after Père Armand saw his first panda, Teddy and Kermit shot one and brought it back to the states. The mountains where the Roosevelts had roamed were now lined with kilns. On the side of the road men and women pounded white rock with sledgehammers, throwing broken hunks into the fires to make lime.

An explosion of dynamite rocked our car. Upstream, a coal mine spewed smoke and dust into a wild river and the vertiginous slopes were bare. Below, tea, rice, and rapeseed were grown, and on midriver islands there were truck farms: cabbages, onions, peas, and beans, but no large trees.

Deforestation had been going on in China since before the Middle Ages. By the fourteenth century, central China was denuded. During Mao's Great Leap Forward from 1957 to 1958, millions of trees were cut down to make charcoal for backyard steel furnaces where pots and pans and Buddhist icons were melted down. This was Mao's strategy to make China a self-sufficient modern nation. Later, the metal was thrown away because it was not strong enough. Women were encouraged to have children and the population increased by 450 million. Schools were closed down. Crops were left to die in the fields while both children and adults attended to their revolutionary activities. The wildlife population was decimated for food, and all arable land was plowed and planted in grain—wheat in the north, rice in the south—crops that were later neglected.

Starvation was so extreme that people ate weeds and sawdust. Grass soup was the soup du jour. Yet Mao saw nothing of it. When his train went through towns and villages where hunger was extreme, his comrades pulled the shades so he wouldn't see, because if he did, they were afraid they would be blamed for the disaster and executed. "I remember, even the worms were hungry. They came up out of the ground and ate everything in the fields and then we all starved," a friend who lived through that era told me.

We followed the Jitiao River up a narrow canyon into the Qiong-lai Mountains, where the pavement stopped and a one-lane track threaded through fallen boulders. The water ran fast and clear and the canyon's narrow verge offered us tantalizing glimpses of high, cloud-ridden peaks ahead. More than once we had to stop as landslides were cleared away. This was the ecotone between the Tibetan plateau and the Sichuan basin, and all this had once been forest: prime habitat for bears, golden monkeys, takin, white-lipped deer, and snow leopards. Even the trees that had been replanted had not been cared for and the regrowth was thick brush, difficult for bears and deer to travel through.

Nature reserves were established in China in 1958, and the first panda reserve in 1963. But their management ended abruptly during the Cultural Revolution and didn't start up again until 1976, when a census of surviving pandas was taken. In the six mountain areas where pandas were known to live, only 1100 animals were counted. At Wolong, where we were headed, only 80 had survived.

How we treat our animals is a mirror of how we think of ourselves. How could one expect a leader who humiliated and enslaved his followers to treat animals well?

Mr. Tong cooly navigated the bumpy Wolong road through herds of goats tended by young boys. He laughed as he told how the year before, a boulder had fallen onto the hood of his truck, then bounced into the middle of the road, stopping all traffic for days. He referred to pandas as *daxiongmao*—"bear-cats"— and said he had lived near here while in cadre school, but never saw a bear.

Pandas are small, shy, slow moving and rather fragile. They are only 15 centimeters long when they're born and weigh from 60 to 130 grams. Their dens are usually rock caves or hollow trees, and they don't breed until they are five years old or more, with estrus lasting only one week per year. Of the seven species of bamboo in Wolong, pandas eat the leaves and young stems of only two: umbrella and arrow. The 1983 flowering and subsequent die-off of arrow bamboo helped decimate their population.

At a bend in the river we turned into the Hetauping Research Center. It consisted of a group of low, flat-roofed cement buildings huddled on the banks of the Jitiao River. We entered through heavy gates, walked over a bridge, and came into the compound. Three young men dressed in sports jackets, jeans, and tennis shoes approached us. I asked if they were biologists. They said no, they were guides. Were there any English-speaking biologists around? They said the Canadian biologist who had been there for four years had left the week before. Now there were no scientists to talk to. But if I wanted, I could look around anyway.

The pandas were held in dirty, cement stalls with stalks of bamboo piled in the corners. Some had small outdoor enclosures but these seemed little used. I looked into the first cage. The panda, a small male, was slouched in the corner, his head hung down low, the bamboo untouched. "He's not eating. Not feel good," the young attendant said disinterestedly, a cigarette hanging from his dry lips. In the next enclosure a female lay on her stomach with her paws over her masked face. "When will they be turned back out into the wild?" I asked. The young man shrugged. "These pandas are here because they are sick." And indeed, they looked sick, but probably from incarceration, not illness.

The eminent biologist and writer, George Schaller, came to Wolong in 1980 to help do fieldwork among the bears. His book, *The Last Panda*, tells of his struggles working and living in a society that values both humans and animals as commodities and where the land's carrying capacity had long been overfull. During Schaller's stay, he railed against the unnecessary capture and long detention of the bears. Now, walking around the compound, it was easy to see that these animals were sacrificial: above their cages were the names of donors to the Research Center. "Donated by Ruby Fielding, lover of wildlife," one of the plaques said. Her "adopted" panda stared at me listlessly, a hostage for raising money. Who knows how the monthly donations were spent?

As I quickly passed by the rest of the cages, I could not help returning to Mao's thoughts on using the atomic bomb. His "paper tiger theory" argued that China could afford to lose millions of people in a nuclear war. What difference did it make, since there were so many? he had said.

In the shop, there were T-shirts, mugs, and postcards for sale. When it became clear that I had no intention of adopting an animal, the attendant lost interest and rejoined his friends who appeared to be employed there, but had nothing to do. Finally, I could not bring myself to look into the eyes of another caged bear, and we departed.

Sick at heart, I wandered the mountains north of town all the next day. We had been staying in a hotel built for foreigners visiting the preserve, but the building had never been finished. Breakfast and dinner were taken in the former hotel complex, but the stench from dirt and grime made it almost impossible to eat. Walking up the hill to the land cruiser after an early breakfast, we ran into the administrators of the preserve. They had just taken their first Western ballroom dancing class the night before. Excited by their new skill, they practiced dancing in the passageway between offices: the tango, the foxtrot, and the waltz. It was six in the morning.

A map of the area, hand-drawn by a British biologist years before, was posted on the bulletin board. It showed a small temple in the mountains nearby. When I asked the dancers if they knew of it, they shrugged and twirled. We drove up the mountain road and stopped to ask a group of men. Finally one of the workers stepped forward, unafraid to speak. He explained that there was an old Tibetan lama up in the hills beyond the fields. The villagers were rebuilding a temple there. He gave us the lama's name and pointed to the mountain. "He's at home now because he's sick. He will talk to you."

On foot we followed a rushing stream up a steep slope between mud-brick houses with flat roofs and terraced gardens of vegetables and rice. Two young women in pink angora sweaters and velvet stretch pants hoed weeds between rows of tomatoes. In another field the older women wore long, homespun blue dresses and white turbans on their heads.

This northwest corner of Sichuan Province on the border of the Tibet Autonomous Region is home to the ancient Qiang minority, a large Tibetan borderland group that had once lived in the northern provinces of Qinghai, Shaanxi, and Gansu. At the end of the Tang dynasty, around 900 A.D., they were defeated in a war over agricultural land and slowly migrated south to the mountains around the Wolong Preserve.

To get from one field to the next we walked the paths between plots, jumping irrigation ditches, then skirted through the yards of villagers' houses. No one seemed to mind our intrusion. In these inner sanctums, bamboo fences enclosed black pigs, guard dogs chained to posts barked as we passed, and chickens on the loose ran for cover.

A raptor had been shot and hung against a red adobe wall to dry; bundles of husked corn swung from hand-carved beams. As we continued up the mountain, a woman in the field stood, looked at us, smiled, and stooped over again, pulling weeds from between hundreds of tomato plants. Above were the high aeries where pandas chewed on bamboo, but at this elevation we stepped on no land that had not been cultivated for thousands of years.

The lama's house—it wasn't really his, but one he shared with a young couple who took care of him—was square, with a dark, low-ceilinged entry that led to four closed doors. A young woman greeted us nervously and told us to wait while she woke the old man who had been taking his afternoon nap. Surprised to see us, she tried to look calm. I told her not to wake him, but she insisted: "He'll want to talk to you."

Above my head a false ceiling of woven bamboo held mounds of dried corn. A cat peered over the edge, then went back to sleep. The dog barked as the old lama stood in the opened doorway, stiff backed and using a cane. Barely five feet tall and barrel-chested, his graying hair was shoved up inside an untidy turban. He wore leggings, a blue coat covered with a goatskin vest, and green tennis shoes. He stopped, looked up into our faces, and gave us a broad, nearly toothless smile.

The young woman motioned us outside into the courtyard and arranged a bench for us, but the lama preferred to sit on a stone and lean against the wall in what was left of the day's light. Lifting his face to the sun, he told me he was eighty years old and not well, though he couldn't say what was wrong with him. There had once been three lamas on this mountain, but now he was the only one left and there was no one to replace him. When he was growing up in this valley there were only eighteen families here.

"In those days there was no road and bandits roamed the mountains. Everyone helped each other," he said. "Now, it's all government. Now, it's hard to survive."

I asked how he became a lama in an area so remote. "My three brothers and I were very poor. We had nothing to eat. So I went to a temple down the mountain and told the lama there I wanted to study with him."

Now all his brothers were dead and he was the only one left in the valley who could read Tibetan. During the Cultural Revolution, his temple was burned down and he hid in this house. "We lived quietly. We practiced quietly; practice was reading sutras," he said. "I also did something bad," he whispered, and a smile came over his face. He motioned to the young husband to get something from the house. A bundle wrapped in old red cloth was laid before me. Inside were Buddhist scriptures written in Tibetan on long narrow sheafs of yellowing paper held between two wooden boards. The lama untied the bundle. Wind picked up a few of the pages and swirled them across the courtyard. When I retrieved them, the paper almost came apart in my hands.

"I hid these during the Cultural Revolution. In this house. If they had been found, I would have been killed," the lama said. I asked him to read one of the sutras. He straightened up and when sound came from his mouth, it wasn't speaking, but song. His wizened face was dark against the stubbled adobe wall and his voice was birdlike. A breeze picked up, the dried corncobs rattled, and the chanting blended into the wind.

We rewrapped the scriptures in the red cloth. The old lama held them between his hands and bowed until his forehead touched the wooden cover. "He sings that way every morning and evening," the young woman said. She had moved to another part of the courtyard where she busied herself drying millet in a flat basket, sifting through the grains with one hand and holding her baby with the other. The lama rolled the unlit cigarette we had given him between his fingers, then asked for a light. The wind kept blowing out the match, which amused him. Finally he inhaled deeply, coughed, and gazed up at the ridge where the new temple was being built.

"I don't understand it. The people who burned the temple down during the Cultural Revolution are the same ones rebuilding it. Why do they bother?" His eyes twinkled and we laughed. Standing to leave I looked at the high peaks behind his house. Had he ever seen any panda bears? He said no, not since he was a child, but he knew of people down in the valley who still shot and ate them.

From my rucksack, I pulled out the oranges we had bought in Chengdu and gave them to the lama. Still gazing at the peaks, he said, "All the Han Chinese live below in the valley. We Tibetans were made to live up here where the soil is no good. They thought they were punishing us, but they don't understand. Up here in the mountains, this is where the spirit lives. Who cares if things don't grow!"

He held an orange up, inspecting its pockmarked skin. "I only want sunshine for everyone," he said with a wry smile. Sun emerged from behind a bank of clouds for the first time all day. Bemused, the old lama laughed, thanked us, then shuffled back into the dark house shaking the bag of oranges as if they were tiny, portable suns by whose light he could read sutras.

The young husband showed us the way to the temple that was being built on the ridge above the lama's house. He was reserved and hardly spoke. We clambered up through more farmland, past three graves, through a small orchard of fruit trees. The townspeople had told the lama they would bring him back to live in the temple when it was finished, but he was skeptical, telling them he probably wouldn't live that long.

We walked along the ridge toward the site. Its *feng shui* was good: on approaching the little flat where reconstruction was taking place, one had a sense of well-being. The temple overlooked the whole valley but could not be seen from the road below. Up behind, a steep vegetated gorge full of wild bamboo and flowering rhododendrons let out a thin trickle of water. In front of the unfinished building, thirty or forty villagers were planing thick beams and carving roof parts. The faces that gathered around us as we approached seemed to represent the entire village: young and old, bright, dumb, shy, and smart-alecky—a miniature portrait of society, including the town idiot and the old sage.

An old woman offered me tea. Her remaining teeth were so loose that they floated in her mouth as she talked and her eyes glistened. The workers carried mountain green tea in jars and sipped it unheated all day. They invited us to see the inside of the temple.

On the bottom floor, a crude altar had been erected with a gold Buddha and a horse with a dragon's head. In the front, pots and bowls held long sticks of incense. The upstairs was strewn with litter from the temple-warming: shells of firecrackers carpeted the floor. One of the young men rooted around until he found a few that had not been lit and the fireworks began all over again. Above my head was the small third story, a room where traditionally the lama slept and sutras were kept safe under a copper roof that shone in the sun.

Chinese buildings are constructed like tables; all the heaviness and structural strength is located at the top, giving a sense of free-floating space and foot room for pilgrims below. The mortise and tenon joints at the roofline take the brunt of the temple's tensions and compressions, with weight bearing down from above on long legs transpierced by hand-hewn horizontal beams. Top-heavy and bandy-legged, a temple might walk away during the night. That's how movable they seem, mirroring two basic tenets of the Buddhist scriptures they house: that the ritual journey or movement on the Path represents *samadhi*; and that while the structure looks permanent, it is not.

Gazing out from this winged temple-perch high on a ridge, I thought how different a Chinese temple was from the heavy-footed cathedrals of the West, whose vaulted arches look toward heaven, but whose soles are cemented into the mud of a patriarchal god and the mire of original sin.

The temple's head carpenter, jauntily dressed in a magenta shirt and leggings, black wool pantaloons, and a blue Mao cap, planed a curve into a roof beam set on two sawhorses. The sledgehammer by his feet was made from a block of wood and a handle trimmed from a tree limb. Among his other tools were chisels, hammers, and small axes. Such iron tools have been made in China since the sixth century B.C.

Even though there had been no public Buddhist practice at this temple since 1949, and no temple reconstruction until the 1980s, traditional building styles had not been forgotten. Is this how a culture recreates itself? Did these villagers care about what they were building, or were they just working for a wage given to them by the same government that had coerced them to burn the temple down? And did that matter, or was it only important that it be rebuilt?

Before leaving we gave money to the construction fund. The villager who kept the books for the project wrote his address in my notebook and instructed me to learn the characters so I could write to them. When I asked how soon the old lama would be reinstated and when regular practice might begin, the villagers looked at each other, shrugged good-naturedly, and said they didn't know. Sipping their green tea, they watched as we left. A few more firecrackers were set off, then work resumed.

In the morning Mr. Tong drove upriver as light filled the canyon. The sun the lama had invoked was there to stay. Two old men squatted by the river in the clear mountain light, brushing their teeth. Their clothes hung on a stick fence to dry. Walls of schist shone silver and the river was molten. Here there were trees; they grew all the way down to the water on steep cliffs and spring gardens were sown on thin gravel bars between rapids. Ricks of split wood were laid against the mud and straw walls of houses whose courtyards were home to pigs, cows, and goats. Where a house was being built, the workers, sleeping in lean-tos, shared a courtyard with the animals.

I wanted to keep driving west into Tibet's high mountains, but Mr. Tong insisted that we turn around as we had no permits for the region ahead. Once before we had been stopped at a roadblock and Mr. Tong had had to show his papers. His air of self-assuredness was tempered with caution. He didn't have to explain why. "Even I'm not allowed to go there," he said.

It was springtime but there were no cleansing winds, no change in weather or temperature. A sameness prevailed. As we descended back toward Chengdu and the luxurious Tibet Hotel, the river widened and basins planted in new crops spread like fat. Along the river's edges, a thick midriff of humans bulged, their thin bodies shaped by generations of hard work, in a country where almost everything, including cement, bricks, roof tiles, chairs, shoes, and clothes, is made by hand.

The rivers ran high. I thought of Mao's fondness for swimming. His trick was to let himself drift downstream with the current. That was also his political style: he seemed to go with the flow of the people, feigning interest in their well-being, but behind the scenes, ruled contemptuously, with an iron hand.

Over and over he swam the great rivers of his country. The difficulty of the river stood for the arduousness of the political change he was insisting upon; but the passivity and self-deception in which he indulged undermined his efforts. Obsessive and messianic, he lacked common sense and compassion, and the brilliance of his ideas quickly foundered. The grave suffering he brought upon his loyal constituents never touched him.

Along the way the river went dry. Then I saw it had been diverted into a long tunnel and released just before the next hydroelectric plant. For a mile the river was running hard and fast, crashing through turbines and set free again, before being sucked into another tunnel. No in-stream flow for this country of fish lovers. A life, or millions of lives were not important here. Mao said, "We always have more."

The old lama had explained. "The Han Chinese are like rivers and so is their thinking. It goes in and out and around. But Tibetans don't do that. We are more like the mountains. We stand up and get straight to the point."

The first small city at the base of the mountains was paralyzed with traffic, and a gray panel of pollution dropped from sky to ground. These were storefront towns—small, look-alike bays with accordioned doors that opened onto the highway. Each one provided an exotic aperçu, a Canterbury tale of life and labor that might help decipher this Chinese world for me. If only we could stop. If only they would talk to me (which they probably wouldn't). If only I understood.

Our land cruiser came to a halt by a store where three bird cages were hanging from the eaves. For a moment the canaries' singing rose up above the sound of traffic. The store next door held a stack of fan belts and dusty distributor caps; in the next bay, a restaurant, a man was eating a bowl of rice; in the next, a man changed the oil in a truck; then another one-room restaurant; and a motorcycle repair shop.

A Qiang woman walked by the long line of trucks and cars carrying a basket of fresh eggs. Behind her, deep inside a hidden courtyard, a row of long blue dresses and turbans dried in the hot sun. A monk on a motorbike squeaked past, head shaved, robes flying, and as we eased forward we passed a bookstore, a food store, a hardware store, and parked trucks loaded down with coal and cement. At the edge of town a Tibetan wanderer carrying a sack over his shoulders walked alongside our car. He was ruddy faced and pigeon-toed and when I suggested we stop and give him a ride, Mr. Tong scowled and shook his head no.

We wound down through foothills. Two children in orange organdy dresses walked hand in hand on the edge of the dusty road, their clothes soiled by soiled air. Here, the river came into confluence with another, the Min River, lined with stone buildings whose balconies housed outdoor kitchens. Woks hanging from hooks swung in the breeze over polluted water. A small mule tiptoed past carrying bundles of bamboo, and women returning from the morning market hefted huge heads of cabbage and sides of pork on their backs, and everywhere the black snowfall of coal dust kept coming down.

Then we were in the country again, where limestone cliffs dwarfed workers. "People work so hard here," I kept saying to Mr. Tong. He smiled. "During the Cultural Revolution people stopped doing everything," he said, "Even farming. All they did was read the sayings of Chairman Mao."

The great river valley of the Min Jiang swallowed us. We were back down in the place that the old lama had described as the "low valley where the Han Chinese live." Street markets lined wide avenues with helter-skelter traffic—the usual array of rickshaws, bicycles, donkeys, and makeshift tractors made with rototiller engines. Looming overhead, a huge billboard advertised the "Qingching American Golf and Country Club" with a crude painting of Arnold Palmer.

Between the edge of one sprawling city and the next were farms. The giant farming communes that had been consolidated under Mao turned out to be unproductive and chaotic. They had been converted back into privately owned rice fields and terraced vegetable farms. A farmer could lease his land, own land and hire tenant farmers—people who farm for others and get half the crop in exchange—or he could farm the land himself. But now, seduced by Deng's "open door policy," many wanted to abandon rural life and go to the cities for jobs. How would China feed itself? I wondered.

For five thousand years, China has maintained a sustainable economy despite its dynastic gyrations. Everything was made in China for China. Now that amazing ingenuity and self-reliance was being traded in for TV sets, Japanese cars, American bathrooms (with no accompanying sewer system), and a chance to join the global marketplace, where almost nobody cared if you were schooled, clothed, or fed, or that you had once been the most sophisticated culture in the world.

Mr. Tong jammed on his brakes to avoid hitting a young couple on a Vespa carrying an oversized lacquered red umbrella. It twirled on its bamboo pole as they swerved, then harness bells rang as two Mongolian ponies pulling a cart full of cut logs trotted alongside our car. I thought of the Dalai Lama's words: "The Earth, our Mother, is telling us to behave. All around signs of earth's limitations abound. If we develop good and considerate qualities within our own minds, our activities will naturally cease to threaten the continued survival of life on Earth. It is important that we forgive the destruction of the past and recognize that it was produced by ignorance."

Passing a small knot of trees near a cluster of L-shaped, thatch-roofed farmhouses, I prayed for the bears of northwestern China and looked for the water ox who, a few days before, had taken his ease in the river. It was almost evening when we passed that same cool spot. Beyond a grove of bamboo rattled against the crumbling adobe walls of a farmhouse. I saw not just one, but six, oxen submerged in a pool of water and the old farmer, squatting on his heels in late afternoon shade, watching his animals cool off.

From

Tian Wen

or

Questions

of Heaven

36

When the Yi shot down the suns, why did the ravens shed
their feathers?

137

King Mu was a breeder of horses. For what reason did he roam
about? What was he looking for when he made his circuit of
the earth?

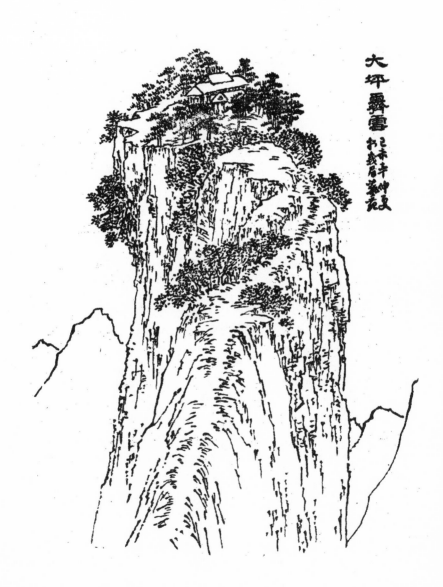

大坪霽雪
己未孟冬神甫

III

Yunnan

The railroad station at Chengdu was a mass of people. Impossible to move without being pressed from in front and behind. An old man's long beard tickled my neck; a beggar appeared from nowhere, thrusting his young head up in front of me, then disappeared. Throngs of men and women from the country, peasants, were lined up waiting to be hired. Drunks lay on the grass while more affluent families going on holiday pushed their hard-sided luggage through the crowds, hitting people in the backs of the knees. Two Tibetans sat on the curb holding a ram's head between them, their human faces much fiercer and wilder than the dead animal's. Others had nothing to sell and were going nowhere. They only waited for an opportunity to make some yuan.

Zhang, the mountain guide who had organized my entire stay in China, had joined me and would be my translator for the rest of the trip. Tall, gaunt, and winsome, he led me through the throng to a quiet waiting room reserved for first-class passengers; he had bought tickets for two sleeping berths on the night train from Chengdu to Kunming.

The compartment was hot but roomy, and quiet since we were its only occupants. The night before at the hotel in Chengdu, Zhang had appeared in the lobby wearing a cowboy hat and the western belt he'd asked me to bring from America. He had just returned from guiding twenty Japanese climbers up

Gongga Shan, a 20,000-foot peak west of Chengdu, and he was slaphappy after downing three Jack Daniels. Married with a young child, he was rarely home. He'd been a river guide in the Canadian Rockies and in Idaho, and these days he took river runners to the head of the Yangtze River on the Tibetan plateau. Now he lay his head back against the soft seat of the train compartment and closed his eyes. His lips were peeling from sunburn and he said he was not happy unless he was on a mountain or a river. "You are a *shan-shui* man," I said. At home on mountains and rivers.

The train trip would take twenty-four hours and even before we left the outskirts of Chengdu, Zhang took on the look of a caged animal, miserable in this rolling zoo. We roared through eight hundred tunnels. The open windows drew in tropically hot air along with soot and dirt that blackened our faces and hands. Three young women conductors, stiff and officious, eyed us coldly and asked for our tickets and passports as if we were crossing into another country. But we were only traveling from one province, Sichuan, to another, Yunnan, in southwest China.

Perhaps the caution was called for since Kunming is now a major city in what's called the "Golden Triangle," consisting of Yunnan and its bordering countries, Myanmar and Laos. Across these borders flows a huge volume of opium and heroin and long lines of stolen, unlicensed cars off-loaded in various ports and driven into China. I had heard about an American businessman whose car had been stolen from his house in Hong Kong. When he went to do business in Shanghai, his would-be Chinese clients picked him up at the airport. He was amazed to see they were driving his stolen Mercedes. Annoyed at first, he played it cool. To make someone lose face in China is serious, so he didn't bring up the subject. Just told them they had a nice car.

.   .   .

The landscape became more mountainous as the train heaved onto the Yunnan plateau. A river gorge narrowed and flared on one side of the train like a skirt torn open by wind. Rickety footbridges swung over rushing water, carrying workers from one field to another, and mounded graves were plugged into untillable hills. "All those graves are for the railroad workers who died building this line," Zhang said between jags of sleep and humming (he was hooked up to his Sony Walkman). "I was dreaming about mountains," he said, closing his eyes. Here, crops terraced the mountains like ladders whose rungs were made of cabbage, bush beans, and peas—an imaginary staircase to Emei Shan's questionable heaven.

Hot and dry. A change in the texture of air woke me. I had been thinking about the *shan-shui* scrolls. The train's movement had become the horizontal unwinding of mountains and rivers under my back. Landscape painting in the Tang and Sung dynasties was intuitive, ecstatic, and momentary. Ssu k'ung-T'u described the process:

> Stoop to get it, there it is;
> Don't go seeking it everywhere
> Move along with the whole Tao
> And a hand's touch creates spring.

Shan-shui represented the two poles of the natural world: mountain is yang, water is yin—male and female, hard and soft, dark and light, death and life. Every brush stroke was a living thing; one movement of the arm could create a whole world.

Brushwork came in many styles. It could be boneless, *mo-ku-hua*—a wash of ink with no outline; or calligraphic, *p'o mu*—a broken rhythm with uneven washes of color. There were dots and strokes, drag strokes, sweeping strokes, back strokes, ink swimming out of a stilled consciousness onto the theatre of silk, rice, and mulberry paper. And painters were always admonished that the landscape and all its parts must first be ingested and internalized: "To paint bamboo, it must first grow in your heart," the adage said.

The literati of Ming dynasty China composed poems and made paintings of the "immortals' land": mountains or island-mountains sticking up out of milky seas. Strangely shaped trees marked places of reverence, and waterfalls emptied out of caves into rivers of clouds, then emerged again. The islands were connected by bridges representing the stages of spiritual practice or one's progress toward heaven after death. In the vertical hanging scrolls the residences of immortals were always humble, diminutive in the context of the mountain, sited reverentially, and hidden in clefts or neatly shelved on a terrace beneath the outflow of a waterfall. The point is, the Chinese were always dreaming of mountains. . . .

A conductor knocked on the compartment door and handed us complimentary toilet kits: a washrag, a toothbrush, and a pink plastic flashlight, the instruments of civilized living. But in Kuo Hsi's time, the finest instruments one could own were the painter's brush and inkstone. "In all cases you should master the brush and not be mastered by it; you should master the ink and not be mastered by it. . . . When someone asks what ink he should use, I answer: 'Use burnt ink, ink that has been kept overnight, receding ink, ink made from fine dust. One is not sufficient. You cannot achieve the desired effect through only one ink.' "

Out the train window, terraced crops were unirrigated seedlings, stranded in dry ground, waiting for the coming monsoons. Nobody in our car knew what the altitude was, but the humidity was gone. The tunnels came so often they worked like blackouts between strobes of sunlight, and as darkness came, the tunnels were blacker than night. Zhang woke and sat on the seat opposite inspecting his sunburned eyes and lips in a mirror. During the Tang dynasty, mirrors—actually rounds of cast bronze with landscapes in relief whose central knob represented a sacred mountain—were called "mirrors of mind illumination" and were thought to reflect both the internal organs of the viewer's body as well as his inner feelings.

We roared through an area of the Yi people, a minority group that lives in the western fringes of these mountains and believes it is descended from birds. The women wore Tibetan-style *chubas* with elaborate, squared-off headdresses, bright as lanterns and as colorful as the heads of birds. In the dusk, children on horses splashed through the river, screaming with delight as their cattle drifted up a green slope toward home. No cars, no roads, just this train intruding. The afternoon had cooled, and flooded terraces mirrored mountain cirques. Red earth deepened to purple and farmers walking home were silhouettes only. Pine smoke replaced coal smoke and an almost full moon blotted out stars. In the *Analects VI*, Confucius wrote: "The man of wisdom delights in water; the man of humanity delights in mountains."

A conductor walked through the train ringing a bell. Time for dinner. We went forward to the dining car. As the door creaked open Chinese disco music blasted out. The room was overbright with neon. The tubular chairs crowded around tables were so flimsy they collapsed under our weight, much to everyone's delight. The wall sconces were chrome and colored glass, almost, but not quite, art deco.

All but one table were full with young couples. This was the first year that city people had been given Saturday off from work. Having enough money and time as well as permission to travel in their own country was still a rare treat. Celebrating, they were chugging beer, eating plates of fish and spitting the bones on the floor. To get to my seat I had to step over piles of spindly carcasses. When our dinner came, Zhang and I couldn't eat it: the fish were nothing but mouthfuls of bones. Instead, we drank beer, ate rice, and longed for the food, whiskey, and wine we'd had at the hotel the night before.

Back in the compartment, Zhang said he wanted to tell me something. He looked around, closed the door, and pulled the blind. During the Cultural Revolution, he said, he had been just a boy and didn't remember the happenings of 1949, when the Communist Party took over from the Nationalists. Nor did he remember the 1957 Mao purge called the Hundred Flowers, the policy of "letting one hundred flowers bloom, one hundred schools of thought contend," during which artists and intellectuals were asked by Mao to freely criticize the government, not realizing they were being tricked. In a series of purges, Mao used their words against them and imprisoned them for being rightists. Later came the killing of 20 million landlords, including monks and abbots of Buddhist monasteries. Then came the fruitless Great Leap Forward, when Mao demanded that people stop all work and do nothing but make steel in their backyard furnaces. As a result, most of China starved.

But Zhang did recall the 1960s when his father, a factory manager, was struggled against, because he and his mother had been forced to watch. "The Red Guards came to the factory and took my father out of his office. They stood him in the courtyard, put a dunce's cap on him, smeared him with excrement, strapped signs on his back that said he was a counterrevolutionary. The workers hit and whipped him and broke his bones.

That afternoon he was demoted and sent away. That's all I remember," Zhang said. "Now I must sleep." He opened the blinds slowly, then hoisted himself in one flying leap onto the top berth. After a long silence in the dark, he murmured, "All I want to do is live in the mountains. That is where I feel alive. That is where I feel at peace."

Sometime during the night we crossed from Sichuan into Yunnan Province. Yunnan means "south of the clouds," and refers to the Himalayas that tower above its western edge. It has always been a multicultural region, home to thirty minority nationalities, including Hui Muslims brought by Kublai Khan as mercenaries seven hundred years ago, and peoples of Tibetan descent: the Yi, Bai, and the matrilineal Naxi who have lived in these mountains for at least two thousand years. Considered barbarous, Yunnan was not even annexed to China until the Ming dynasty (1368–1644).

At one in the morning the train screeched to a stop. We both woke and looked out. It was a small town and as passengers were boarding, Zhang and I got off to stretch our legs. On another track peasants were climbing onto the tops of freight cars of a train going in the opposite direction. How would they survive all those tunnels, I wondered. Engineers walked the length of our train tapping the couplings with hammers. Having seen vendors, Zhang ran off trying to find something good to eat. By the side of the tracks workmen huddled by small fires, warming their hands. When the conductors made the announcement to board the train, I looked but could not find Zhang, and not knowing what else to do, got on without him.

What was I doing here? By the time I'd climbed up and back down Emei Shan during my first four days in the country, I'd felt a sense of defeat. I had been naive about the extent of the destruction during the ten-year-long Cultural Revolution. Almost everything spritual, intellectual, and creative was purged and erased; the heart was ripped out of the culture and its people. Beauty had been considered a mockery by the Maoists; no corner in Han China seemed to offer any gracenotes, and I felt profoundly sad. Consoling myself, I read a poem by Su Shi:

> From the traveler, singing: from the field, weeping—both
> spur sorrow.
> Fires in the distance, dipping stars move slowly toward
> extinction.
> Am I waiting up for New Year's? Aching eyes won't close.
> No one here speaks my dialect: I long for home.

When Mr. Tong had driven me to Su Shi's house in Meishan, south of Chengdu, he'd gotten lost. Not many of his clients wanted to go there. The house and grounds have been made into a theme park; we paid the usual entry fee and were handed our tickets. Su Shi, also known as Su Tung-p'o, was born during the Sung dynasty. From his house he could see the gold peaks of Emei Shan. At age twenty, Su Shi took the formidable Jinshi exam and placed second; a few years later he took a higher exam and received the highest honors ever given in the empire, married a fifteen-year-old girl and went off on his first statesman's job. During the next forty years he lost two wives, was banished and reinstated by numerous emperors, was exiled three times, farmed a hardscrabble piece of land and studied Zen. More often, he called himself a *Yu Fan*: "One who had been slandered and wrongfully banished to the south and who had never received the pardon he deserved."

Longing for home, traveling from place to place, Su Shi was never a stranger. Throughout those difficult years he wrote elegant poems and painted landscapes employing the free-flowing brushwork for which he became famous. He wrote about the art of calligraphy, performed civic duties, helped the poor and sick, drank wine with monks and friends, and died just after his banishment had ended. He was arriving home. His last poem:

> Bell and drum on the south river bank:
> home! I wake startled from a dream.
> Drifting clouds—so the world shifts;
> lone moon—such is the light of my mind.
> Rain drenches down as from a tilted basin;
> poems flow out like water spilled.
> The two rivers vie to send me off;
> beyond treetops I see the slant of a bridge.

All through China's five-thousand-year history, there have been waves and waves of exile and redemption, feast and famine, chaos and renaissance. There have been uprisings, ethnic cleansings, famines, religious persecutions, and returns to cultural glories and peace, followed by catastrophic dynastic change. Books had been burned in 213 B.C. When the emperor Shih Huang-ti destroyed the records of the past and then encircled and isolated his people with the Great Wall, he melted down their instruments of warfare to make two huge statues that he hoped would scare away invaders from the north. Realizing that he was mortal and might not live to see the fruition of his newly purged empire, he sent shamans to find the cure for mortality. They searched for years, finally finding a medicinal plant they thought would prolong his life. But when they administered the potion, the emperor promptly died. The Ch'in Dynasty gave way to the Han, and culture was restored.

The latest dynasty to collapse was Mao's. "In the end, he was just another emperor," a Chinese friend remarked. I asked another question of heaven: Could this culture be restored yet again?

Out the train window I saw people working hard to get a footing in a vascillating political climate, a bed of quicksand whose ground rules change with the wind. "We have all betrayed each other until no one knows how to tell the truth," a friend who had been a Red Guard told me. The stern, suspicious silence of the older people stopped me; the desperate materialism of the young gave me the compulsion to talk to them about the Holocaust. I kept reminding them about remembering to remember so that bad things would not happen again. But Zhang said the young people know nothing about the old culture of China: "They don't care that it is gone."

I looked down the aisle. Still no Zhang. What would I do if he had missed the train, with my tiny Chinese dictionary whose pronunciation guide was for Beijing Chinese, a dialect so different from the one spoken in Yunnan, it might have been another language altogether? The train jerked into motion and I fell back onto my seat. Fingering my round-the-world plane ticket, I knew I could be in Sydney, Paris, New Delhi, or London by the end of the next day. For a moment I almost hoped Zhang wouldn't reappear. Then he did, smiling wryly as if he'd meant to scare me, holding out a Chinese-style burrito and a large bottle of beer.

As we began our descent from the mountains, the image of Yi villages threaded together only by footpaths stayed in my mind. Not that they hadn't been affected by the dispiteous anarchism of the Cultural Revolution, but they lived in relative isolation. The gaudiness of the Yi peoples' clothes seemed a remnant of a rich cultural past at odds with the reductive plainness of Han China today.

Now pine smoke from the mountains mixed with the scent of cut straw. In the moonlight I saw a lone Yi woman, top-heavy with headdress, raking hay by moonlight, speared by the passing strobe of our train.

From

Tian Wen

or

Questions

of Heaven

83

When the Great Turtle walks along with an island on his back,
how does he keep it steady?

寒池直月
蘇甫仲夜
蔵

IV

—

Lijiang

In the morning our train arrived in the southwestern city of Kunming and we met our new driver, Feng. Small and stoop shouldered, he jammed us and our camping gear into his VW with a nervous sweetness. We were going to the once isolated town of Lijiang on the border between Han China and Tibet, to Peter Goullart's *Forgotten Kingdom*, to Joseph Rock's Nancho Kingdom, to the World War II Flying Tigers' airbase, to Shangri-la, the town on which James Hilton based his lost paradise.

All roads to paradise first pass through purgatory. But before leaving Kunming, we stopped to eat. In the street markets between the usual pens of live snakes, chickens, turtles, eels, and fish, we bought fresh bananas, oranges, and Asian pears and went to a small corner restaurant to fill up on a Kunming specialty: noodles in red pepper broth so hot (in both ways) it cooked the slivers of meat and fish dropped into it.

Kunming's gracious, semitropical, tree-lined avenues were chockablock with small shops, all selling cheap American-style clothes and Japanese toys. One storefront turned out to be a miniature hospital. Open to the street were four beds, three of them occupied by patients, with a doctor and nurse administering IVs as pedestrians, bicycles, motorbikes, taxis and trucks roared by.

The trip to Lijiang from Kunming would take seventeen hours by car and we had already been twenty-four hours on the train. During World War II, Kunming had been General Stilwell's base, the jump-off place for moving supplies over the hump in Burma. The first leg of our trip from Kunming to Dali would follow that historic road.

I watched Feng's soft, twitching, apologetic face in the rearview mirror as we headed out of the city. He had rolled his pant legs shin-high before slipping into the cramped driver's seat as if in preparation for the wild ride to come. And wild it was. Feng drove maniacally, impatiently, honking his horn every few seconds, alternately jerking forward and slamming on his brakes as we threaded our way through Chinese gridlock. I closed my eyes and prayed for the cool, streetwise Mr. Tong to reappear at the wheel, but he did not. The oranges and apples I had bought rolled like billiard balls, hitting the back of my head. Zhang put on his earphones and closed his eyes.

I had been reading *Forgotten Kingdom*, a memoir about Lijiang written by Peter Goullart, an ebullient Russian who escaped with his mother during the Revolution and landed in Shanghai. When his mother died in 1924, Peter was already fluent in Chinese, had spent time in a Taoist monastery, and landed a much needed job with the Chinese government setting up local crafts cooperatives in remote parts of China. His work eventually led him to the isolated mountain town of Lijiang.

He wrote: "The prospect of travelling on the Burma Road filled me with dread. This great highway, although marvelously constructed, well kept and extremely picturesque, has been a notorious killer. It climbs several mountain ranges of about 10,000 feet by a series of hairpin turns and runs along the edge of giddy precipices . . . I can never forget the sight of countless heavy trucks lying at the bottom of deep ravines, smashed beyond salvage."

Narrow and unshouldered, the road to Lijiang was an unruly ribbon that pulled over the accordioned landscape, mountain pass after mountain pass, some as high as 13,000 feet. The turns were sharp and the way was vertiginous, and every switchback was the scene of an accident: a whole wheel spun off the axle of one logging truck, while another lost its load in the center of the road. Yet another truck had tumbled over a verge just before we passed by. Not much had changed since Peter Goullart had passed through fifty years before.

To distract myself, I studied a map. The Yunnan plateau is a series of steps descending from the Himalayas. Long ropes of northwest-southeast ranges curve down, with deep river valleys between. At the lower elevations the mountains are dry with red soil and scrub pines, their streams bordered by bamboo. At times the vegetation looked like California's: eucalyptus and sycamore trees gave shade to hard-used humans and animals, and bougainvillea crawled up the adobe walls of the Yi houses.

The literature of travel in ancient China represents a spatial progression through a string of spheres linked by a single road: we sped across range after range, valley after valley. Time was demarked in ancient travelogues by what is called the "hoary stems" system: each year, month, and day was denoted using two characters—one heavenly, the other, earthly—with the cycle repeating after sixty combinations, linear sequences within recurring cycles describing the permutations of heaven and hell.

The road we took that morning, the Burma Road, began to feel like such a cyclical path: time swirled as the alpine glories of each mountain range were defiled by terror. In my library at home I had looked at a Lijiang shaman's scenes of hell. Called the *Dongba's Road Map*, it showed scenes of dread, the lower and middle realms full of "demons, torturers, civil magistrates, and humans."

The car swerved and straightened and I thought about other scenes of literary purgatory: the sixth book of Virgil's *Aeneid*, the circumambulations in Seamus Heaney's *Station Island*, the cold *bardos* of the *Tibetan Book of the Dead*. To get to paradise, or to enlightenment, one must first go through the initiatory rites; one must become dead before waking. As we drove I thought of Virgil's lines in the *Aeneid*: "Souls for whom a second body is in store: their drink is the water of Lethe, and it frees from care in long forgetfulness."

How many mountains had we crossed and how many rivers? I longed to be freed from care and would have welcomed a bottle of tequila. Villages merged one into another as we sped through, always too fast, Feng's hand always on the horn. Five slaughtered pigs lay in a row by the side of the road—for sale, Feng told me. Around another mountain peasants threw sheaves of grain onto the asphalt, letting our rolling tires thresh it for them. After we passed, the peasants quickly swept up the loosened grain with bamboo brooms. Everywhere animals were tied up except for the gangs of goats on the side of the highway. They ate anything green that had not already been eaten by humans. Men, women, and children planted rice seedlings in straight lines marked by strings stretched across the field which were moved each time a row was completed. The foothills and mountains had been clear-cut and the standing windbreaks of eucalyptus trees were sheared of their arms. Insecticide sprayed from backpacks glistened on the dull frosting of night soil, and women bent down into the mud of the paddy, their hoes slick with water and earth.

Some of the women coming from the fields had black eyes and bandaged legs. "What happened to them?" I asked Zhang. "They've been beaten by the men who hired them," Zhang said, then turned his head away. "The women who need work go to the city's labor pools where these men bring them back to the country, rape and beat them, and make them work the fields."

Zhang slept again, Feng smoked, and I opened the windows to keep from getting carsick. I thought of the prostitutes I had seen on the planes and in the hotel lobbies. Mao had insisted that men stop beating their wives. He admired women, reminding the men that women "hold up half the sky." Bride prices, female slavery, binding of feet, prostitution, child marriages, and female infanticide were all prohibited. But since the 1980s, equality for women seems to be a thing of the past. No women hold important political or business offices. Their feet are not bound, but the poor and uneducated are often traded and used in any way desired. In 1993 a group of men who traded in women, were caught by police; they had already abducted 1,800 women from the Beijing labor market and sold them in a distant province. In some villages retarded women are bought for cash or in exchange for a horse or pig. They are prized because they obey, bear children, and work hard in the fields. The killing of female babies, with its long history in China, is also on the rise again. It's reported that since 1990, a million baby girls go missing each year.

We drove through high mountain villages where women held up long skeins of garlic. After a long silence, Feng woke Zhang to translate for him so he could tell me the story of his life. He had been born in Kunming but during the Great Leap Forward he was sent to a labor reform camp near what was then the Burmese border and stayed for eighteen years. The famine had just begun and he went hungry along with millions of others. He hated country life and was often beaten. In 1976 he was allowed to return to his hometown. There was no work and his wife left him. Their child was raised by her grandmother. "It's not the work that was hard, it was to be hungry," he said, sipping from his ever present jar of green tea.

We passed an overloaded truck that had tipped into a ditch and had come to rest against a tree. The drivers, apparently expecting no help for a while, were making beds under a gray tarp beneath the back of the overhanging load. Moving uphill towards a blind hairpin turn, Feng suddenly accelerated. It took me a moment to understand what he was doing: he was trying to pass the truck in front of us as a logging truck on the other side was coming downhill toward us. I screamed into his ear: "NO!" He was so shocked his foot went for the brake and we were saved. Then he complained to Zhang that I shouldn't disrupt his driving.

On the next pass he tried it again and I yelled at Zhang that I wanted to stop, get out, and walk to Lijiang. Both men laughed at me and Feng continued at breakneck speed through the middle of villages, honking down horse carts and women burdened with baskets of vegetables. Surely this would be over soon. I was nauseous and asked again to stop. Finally Feng pulled up to a roadside restaurant. While he was outside at the communal bathroom, Zhang explained to me that Feng was fragile, that he had a drinking problem, that he had been suicidal—Zhang's way of consoling me. What made me feel even sicker was the thought of having to return to Kunming from Lijiang on this same road.

Feng emerged from the kitchen, having ordered for us since he was familiar with Yunnan cuisine. He had a sweet, fussy way of inspecting the food and insisted that we finish everything on our plates—advice from a man who had known starvation. Before the food came, he sat on the floor at a low table and ordered a water pipe, a hookah, which he lit and inhaled deeply. "Is that opium?" I asked Zhang. (Not an outrageous question since opium has become popular again.) He assured me it was tobacco, which the Yi people grow in these mountains as a crop and store in square towers along the road. Feng was a low altitude man, a driver used to the benign indolence of Kunming and the countryside south which borders Vietnam. "He's tired and doesn't want to go to sleep at the wheel," Zhang explained.

The food was green soybeans, broth with chopped up animal parts whose shapes resembled something out of the Burgess Shale, slivers of bacon, and onions swimming in rancid rapeseed oil. A cop car flashed by, then an ambulance with a battered front fender and a smoking radiator as if carrying victims from its own accident. We had already been driving seven hours and when I asked how much longer we had to go, the sky lowered down with a soft drizzle and Feng looked up and shrugged. All I could think of was how slippery the roads would be in the rain.

Looking around, I wondered where the heaven was located to which one addressed such questions. Instead, I thought of the questions I'd asked an environmental consultant to the World Bank. We'd met at a hotel while feasting on rabbit burgers and beer. He had an all-American face and build and sandy hair, but having been educated at the London School of Economics, he spoke with the deadpan wit of the Brits. When I told him I'd just climbed Emei Shan, he looked out the window at a twenty-story high-rise: the Communist Party's new building. "That's the new Emei Shan," he said.

He had been working on water quality issues with the Chinese. For example, Kunming is a city of 1.8 million people and has no sewer system. Raw sewage along with heavy metals and phosphates from numerous factories upstream are dumped into the river and the reservoir used for the city's domestic water supply. There were no water treatment plants and if the Chinese did not purify the city's water, the algae in the reservoir would become so dense the water would be absorbed in their sponge. The city of Kunming would be waterless by the year 2000. In response, the Chinese had done nothing.

Still driving. Darkness infiltrated polluted skies and the road glistened. I'd had face-offs with death more than once and knew I didn't want to die on a remote road in a police state at the hands of a man whose mind had been shattered by hardships and famine. Any place but here, I whispered to myself, then tried to make a stupid pact with Feng: if he would slow down, I would buy him whatever he wanted in Lijiang. He shook his head modestly but his foot was less heavy as we climbed into ever higher mountains during the night.

It was eleven P.M. when we arrived in Dali. Because I had been moving for thirty-four hours, the inertia of my hotel bed constituted another kind of oscillation, a pitch and roll of gratitude that I had survived the ordeal of the road.

Dali marked the end of the Burma Road. The next day was the Butterfly Festival, which we missed because no one would tell us when it began or ended. But there had been traditional dances by one of the minority groups who lived in Dali, the Dai, whose everyday dress and headdress were even more elaborate and colorful than those of the Yi; we saw them swarming home on foot and in horse-drawn carts with bells on the harnesses all morning.

Apart from the festivities, Dali looked like a drug smuggler's haven, full of European and American rebels-without-a-cause who spoke Chinese. I hated the place despite its beguiling pagodas and a cerulean lake spreading out before the town in a wide valley. We moved on.

Again I begged Zhang to tell Feng to drive more slowly, which Zhang refused to do, since, he said, it would make Feng lose face in front of me. I was going to say that losing face was better than being dead, but realized the remark would fall on the deaf ears of a man contemplating suicide.

During lunch I had asked Feng why he hadn't run away from his labor reform camp and crossed the border into Myanmar, what was then Burma. He said Burma was worse. No food at all, and anyway, the villagers would have turned him in to the authorities. I looked heavenward and asked this question: Where does one find sanctuary in such a place? Then my question was answered.

We descended through a roof of clouds illuminated by moonlight."The air was like champagne . . ." Peter Goullart exclaimed when he topped out on the ridge overlooking the valley surrounding Lijiang. Jade Snow Mountain loomed silver and snow banners flew from its 18,000-foot peak. Lijiang was embraced by mountains: everywhere white peaks rose up like picket fences, small villages and monasteries dotted the foothills, with the coil of a river wound through. Everywhere there were orchards of peach and almond trees and inside were flowers: peonies and roses climbing broken adobe walls.

The Valley of Horses, as Lijiang was sometimes called, is home to a small minority group of 200,000 people called the Naxi (pronounced "Nashi"). Descended from a Tibetan group, the Qiang (whom I'd seen cultivating their fields in Wolong), they are jolly, vivacious, and ruddy faced. Traditionally, the

Naxi women run the markets, do all the business, herd the horses, and tend the fields, while the men care for babies, play music, and write poems.

Lijiang's ancient center, called Dayan, is a tight-knit village of tile roofs, cobblestone paths, and wandering canals lined with stone houses and stores. Blessedly off limits to automobiles, the small shops sell food, clothes, hardware, medicine, local carvings and paintings, cigarettes, sweets, and liquor. All walkways eventually give onto a small, stone-paved square where Tibetans set up stands to sell food and goods. "The Chinese wanted to take all this down and build high-rises," a resident painter told me. "But we Naxi said no. And they left it. Now they are glad because they have seen that what is a national treasure to us is a tourist attraction to others. They can have their fancy Western hotels."

The name *Lijiang* means "Beautiful River," and the river is the Yangtze, whose source was only recently found high on the Tibetan plateau by a French archeologist. Now the exquisite old town is surrounded by post-Communist urban sprawl which quickly becomes horse pastures and hay fields again.

Tibetans once ruled western China. During the Tang Dynasty they broke through the borders of Han China and raided the ancient capital of Chang'an. The Naxi came from the northeastern highlands of Tibet and took over the rich farming valleys where the indigenous P'ouy had always lived, forcing them up into the gorges and mountains above the Yangtze River and its tributaries, and keeping the well-watered and fertile plain for themselves. When the Tibetans lost the ground they had gained in China, they, too, retreated to the high plateaus.

In 1253 Khublai Khan invaded the western edge of what is now Yunnan Province, which had not been considered a part of the Middle Kingdom of China. The great Khan took over the

Kingdom of Muli to the north but bypassed Lijiang because the Naxi king had paid homage to him in advance, knowing that the Khan's armies invaded only those who resisted him. That's been the hallmark of the Naxi people from the beginning: by being savvy and wise, cheerful and accommodating, they have kept their forgotten kingdom out of the fray.

Until 1949, when the Communist Party took over, Lijiang was a place where life was lived exuberantly. It was a favorite destination of Tibetans, a trading and arts center, the last major town on the caravan route to Lhasa, a place of tolerance and gaiety. The Naxi, numbering around fifty thousand and growing, are dark skinned with broad faces and easy smiles. They speak their own language, as well as Mandarin and Tibetan, and the small temples that dot the mountains just below snowline are painted gold and red—Tibetan in architecture and religious practice.

This valley was so isolated from the rest of the world that the lifeways of the people were never properly collected. Copious notes about Naxi rituals and the Dongba religion were made by Joseph Rock, an Austrian-American botanist and explorer who lived in Lijiang for almost thirty years. But they failed to include a sense of how ceremony and daily life merged. Only Peter Goullart's exuberant memoir of his ten years in Lijiang gives us a taste of how life was lived, of Tibetan merchants and lamas coming and going on the much traveled caravan route to Lhasa; of the ease and timelessness of village life; of Dongba shaman exorcisms and lovers' suicides; of tea shops and music concerts and parties.

I had been told to look up a musician and ethnomusicologist in Lijiang named Xuan Ke. Thinking it would be difficult to find him I prepared myself for the usual rounds of questions and suspicions encountered elsewhere. Instead, the first person we asked said sweetly, "He lives just around the corner. In fact, there he is!"

A small-framed, handsome man approached. He had a square-cut face and sensuous lips and when I introduced myself, he smiled, holding out both hands in greeting. He spoke fluent English and didn't care that I was a friend of a friend of his: he simply welcomed me. All I knew about him was this: once a student of piano and conducting at the conservatory in Kunming, Xuan Ke spent twenty years in jail, from 1958 to 1978, and the scars on his wrists from the torture he endured there still showed.

"Now I have been a free man almost as many years as I was jailed," he said, as if astonished at his own realization. "If a man has a hard life at first, then the future is good. Now at sixty-six, I even have a ten-year-old daughter!" he said as we walked. He stopped to turn into a house. "Please come hear our music tonight. Seven o'clock." Then he was gone.

In the afternoon we picked up our Naxi translator, Si Wenfeng, a young woman born in Lijiang who wanted to be a tourist guide. On our way to a mountain monastery where she knew the lama, she told me that her name means "wisdom peaks." We drove through foothill villages where wild rose bloomed and wide fields were crowded with mares and newborn foals. Looking out the back window of the car, I could see the central knot of Lijiang: its angled roofs made a design like the Tibetan knot of eternity. Ahead of us, to the north, were the white winding mountains after which Si Wenfeng had been named.

High up in the foothills, at 10,000 feet, Feng decided his small car could go no further, so we walked the red clay road the rest of the way. Ahead we could see a triangular peak with a dark fold down the middle like the central rib of a leaf. "Under that mountain is where the monastery lives," Si Wenfeng said. At a bend in the road we helped a farmer pull a horse-drawn cart out of a bog and in thanks he gave us a ride.

"Under construction" might have been a better name for China. Even this obscure temple was being rebuilt. Young Naxi men were cutting boards and poles with handsaws and inside the temple monks were cutting up pieces of paper on which sutras had been printed. These were rolled, tied with red string, and placed inside pottery statues of bodhisattvas, newly made. "We put the sutras inside the heart, forever to stay there," a doe-eyed young man said.

Another monk who spoke only Tibetan sat on the floor next to the statues and, with his fingers, made a series of graceful gestures called *mudras*—the Dharmachakra *mudra* and the Vitarka *mudra*—which signify the turning of the wheel of the Dharma. These gestures are practiced in order to link the physical with the spiritual, the body and the mind, with no discursive thought between. "I want to make sure the hands of these statues are right," he said. "That's why I am practicing hard."

The head lama of the monastery entered. For a long time he watched the young monk practicing *mudras*. His face was leathery and he had the sharp, clear eyes of a wily animal. When Si Wenfeng greeted him it was obvious that they were old friends. Her family came often to this temple. When we were introduced he said that many people from America had visited him and they were all Buddhists. "You too?" he asked, and I nodded. "Meiguo. Fojiao," I said. ("American. Buddhist.") He laughed at my two words of Chinese and his eyes twinkled. He flirted with the lovely Si Wenfang, then offered Zhang a pinch of snuff from a jade vessel hung around his neck on a gold chain. "From Madras, India," he said proudly, though he confessed he had never been there.

We went down to the monastery shop where the lama coveted an old pocket watch. When I offered to buy it for him, the young salesman said it wasn't for sale. Laughing, the lama pocketed it anyway. Back up in the meditation hall we watched the lama and his monks roll sutras and place them inside the statues. I asked if there were any monks living in the mountains nearby, hermits in the tradition of Milarepa (a Tibetan saint who lived alone in icy Himalayan caves practicing *tummo*, the ability to generate inner heat). The old lama's eyes brightened. "Yes," he said, then paused. "Five hundred years ago there was such a hermit. He lived above this monastery, just two hours walk from here. The hut he lived in was very small. He slept sitting up and didn't eat. Only nettles, just like Milarepa."

Five hundred years. He'd talked about the hermit as if he were still alive and showed me one of the statues in the hermit's likeness. I asked the lama if he had been to the hermit's hut. He said no, but that a visiting Rinpoche had walked to the spot not long ago. When I inquired about how I might find the path, he asked one of the young monks. The monk shook his head. He wasn't sure but gave vague directions which made me wonder if there might not be a hermit living there now. I gave the requisite donation, did three prostrations, and said good-bye.

Walking off the mountain late that day, we were joined by a herd of mares and foals. Two Naxi women in long blue dresses walked behind the animals, idling on their way home. This was the Valley of Horses: as I looked out across the basin below I saw pastures full of mares, geldings, foals, and mule colts everywhere. Watching the two Naxi women amble down a steep path into their village, Si Wenfeng said: "The Naxi are a matriarchal society. The women are in charge of things except that when we marry, we go to live at our husband's parents' house, not the other way around. Naxi men are lazy. Naxi women do all the work, and make all the decisions. Without us they would have nothing; they would starve."

Feng waited for us at the bottom of the hill in his slick-soled city shoes and cardigan sweater. Driving back to Lijiang he honked his horn incessantly as villagers shot dirty looks at us. They were bringing in the last of the unplanted seedlings and harvesting enough food for the evening meal. Some women led mares toward home with young foals following. The colts gamboled down into an irrigation ditch, then shot across the road and down into another. Feng lay on his horn and when one of the young horses didn't move, he hit him in the hock with the car. I screamed in protest, to no avail. He only laughed at me. But the horse, a good-sized stud-colt, kicked back, deeply denting the car door. I gave a loud cheer.

Fifty years ago pigs ran loose in Lijiang streets and the diet was decidedly Tibetan. Caravans brought yak butter tea, roast mutton, *tsampa* (barley), and *chang* (barley beer), and in social and sexual matters, a Tibetan-style joie de vivre reigned.

At the Din Din Cafe, Zhang talked to the owner's daughter who tantalized him with her tight blue jeans, black boots, and American cigarettes. While dinner was being cooked, she set up shots of Johnny Walker Red at the stand-up Western-style bar, while Feng made the rounds of the shops to buy a local brand of booze, which turned out to be pure grain alchohol. The first good meal I'd had in China was in that cafe. The only hazard was the pet turkey who roamed loose and cleaned your plate if you weren't vigilant.

The food was pan-fried soft noodles with vegetables, a plate stacked with pork chops, fresh steamed vegetables and rice, and the last course, which in China is always soup. My traveler's mirth was enhanced by the discovery of Dynasty wine, a dry red from a northwestern province. At seven o'clock, we went to hear Xuan Ke and his orchestra of Naxi musicians.

We reached the hall where the orchestra performed through a gate in a crumbling stone wall. It looked like a bombed-out school house, its dark recesses lit by candles. Metal folding chairs had been set up and soon enough they were filled with travelers—Germans, Australians, Brits, Canadians, and a few Chinese. The cost of admission was only ten yuan and concerts were given every other night all spring and summer. The musicians ambled in with cigarettes hanging from their lips. Coughing and spitting, they slowly tuned their ancient instruments.

Peter Goullart wrote: "When I was in Lijiang sacred concerts were usually held at some rich man's house. At intervals food and drinks were served to both the participants and the guests. The musical sessions were long and arduous but everybody was happy and attentive. The instruments were carefully arranged in a long room, sometimes in the enclosed veranda, and the atmosphere was reverent and definitely religious, with the scent of incense burning in great brass burners . . . The old musicians, all formally dressed in long gowns and makwas, took their seats unhurriedly, caressing their long white beards."

Now there was no rich man's house, no food and drink at intermissions, no costumes. The orchestra was made up of peasants and middle-class Chinese, twenty or thirty of them, dressed in American-style clothes or blue Mao suits. One elderly musician's frail frame was bent almost double and another was tall and gaunt with a white beard that reached to the middle of his chest.

When all the candles were lit, Xuan Ke stood and spoke to the audience in a carefully modulated voice, soft but powerful: "Music is medicine. It can bring life or death. Both players and listeners must always be careful!"

As night came on, the room dimmed and candlelight was obscured by swirling cigarette smoke. Xuan Ke described the instruments of Dong Jin, or Taoist music in the ensemble: the *dizi* and *bobo*, flutes; the *pipa* and *sugudu*, pipes; the *sanxian* and the *guzheng*, strings; the *huqin*, a bowed string instrument; drums, cymbals, and clappers, *tishou*; *muyu*, a globular wooden fish; and the beautiful cloud gongs, *yunluo*.

Next, Xuan Ke introduced the players starting with the oldest and most venerated: Sun Ziming, tiny, wizened, born in 1913, had begun studying music at age fourteen and was skilled at most of the instruments in the orchestra. By trade a traditional paper cutter, he now played the cloud gongs. Zhou Yin Xian, 81, tall and lean with a white beard that reached his waist. Once a caravan driver on the southern Silk Road between Chengdu and Lhasa, a round-trip that took seven months. Along the way, he learned Tibetan songs and later became interested in playing music. He Linghan, born in 1930, potbellied and world weary, played in the local opera company as a teenager, and worked as an accountant. He Hongzhang, 1930, was accomplished on all the plucked and bowed string instruments and had been a member of the orchestra since the 1940s. Chen Qiuyuan, 1937, played the drums, cymbals, and some string instruments. Yang Zenglie, 1939, handsome and gentle, was a professional musician, as well as being a published scholar on ancient music, and played all the instruments in the orchestra. Wang Chaoxin, 1954, a happy-go-lucky pig farmer who played flutes, strings, and the *bili* (a Naxi flute) for local dances; Niu Shiguang, 1964, learned the plucked lute from his father who also had been a member of the orchestra; and Huang Limei, the youngest, born in 1974, and the only woman, played the *guzheng*, a zither. "We call her our escapee from karaoke," Xuan Ke said. "She's not like other young people. She believes in real Chinese music. She's very serious." Then he introduced himself, Xuan Ke, 1930, next to the oldest, plays bowed string instruments and tries to bring Dong Jin music to the world.

Sometimes funny, sometimes serious, Xuan Ke asked us to close our eyes: "It is important to quiet your mind and let the music enter you. Do not think of other things, please." After a long silence, he asked us to watch as he pointed to places on his body where the music might enter: between the eyebrows, in the palms of the hands, the solar plexus, behind the knees, on the bottom of the feet. "If the music is allowed to enter you, you will become healed. Look at us! We are never sick in Lijiang!" Xuan Ke exclaimed, laughing, as the musicians behind him coughed. "Now you will hear our music from South of the Clouds."

He hit a large gong and silence fell over the crowd. Picking up his tiny two-stringed instrument, Xuan Ke quietly motioned for the playing to start. In a tremulous voice the old paper cutter chanted the title of the first song: "wu hu oo ii." The song was called "Eight Trigrams," with words taken from the *I Ching*. A sound rose up: an insistent, plangent wall of human voices, cymbals, gongs, drums, and string instruments, some plucked, others bowed, all gyrating together in a slow, sonorous, squeaking, groaning, pots-and-pans surge, punctuated by a deep-cadenced drum and the sudden slurry of cymbals, like heavy-limbed horses walking. The texture of the music was heterophonic, all melodies followed the same tune, with each strand embellished slightly differently so that a repetitive complexity emerged. Then sharp, high, wavering voices came in—

the singing was shrill—until hand cymbals and the fish-shaped drum sounded, and the gong rang, then the handheld temple bell, bringing the piece to an end.

After "Eight Trigrams," we heard "Waves Washing the Sand," "Ten Offerings to the Gods," and "The Song of the Water Dragon." Each piece had a distinct orchestration yet there was a sameness throughout, the music having emerged from a place and time more homogeneous than ours. The heavy-footed rhythm moved forward, punctuated with bells and percussion, aerated by high cheeping flutes, and I was brought back to earth again by the rich resonance of the Chinese zither.

My eyes were closed and sounds entered me in elliptical sequences like Chinese narrative, recurring cycles and spheres oscillating within more spheres. When Peter Goullart heard these same tunes sixty years before, played by the parents and grandparents of some of these musicians, he wrote: "It was majestic and inspiring and proceeded in falling and rising cadences. Then, as a climax, the great gong was struck. I have never heard in China such a deep and sonorous gong . . . It was a recital of cosmic life as it was unfolding . . ."

What I was listening to was a living tradition of folk and ceremonial music from eighth- and ninth-century China, a tradition that had been squelched and revived several times, once when Confucius's books of music were burned, and again during the last siege of the Cultural Revolution when traditional music was completely disallowed. Now this ancient art was being revived in a remote corner of a wide mountainous land, and for the first time during my stay in China, I knew I was seeing a fragment of culture, like a very sick patient, being brought back to life.

"Someday the world will know a tribe called the Naxi. After

so many years of no freedom, I am hurrying to preserve our culture." Xuan Ke said. "So much ruined, so much lost. I hope I am not too late. This kind of music brings all listeners and all players into harmony with nature, eliminating noise and war while promoting peace. It is music that comes from an expression inside the heart, which is what makes it truly religious."

The next day I visited Xuan Ke at his house. His young daughter sang in the courtyard. Up stairs so steep and narrow a fat person might not have fit, I found myself in Xuan Ke's tiny book-lined study. He lay Bruce Chatwin's book of essays, *What Am I Doing Here*, on my lap, and opened it to the pages written about Lijiang. Then he showed me other books friends had sent in German, English, French, and Chinese. Xuan Ke's taste was eclectic: he read poetry, musicology, novels, essays, his tape deck piled high with classical music both Western and Eastern—the very music, he said, that had kept him alive during his twenty years in prison. "Every day I hummed that music to myself inside my head. It kept the demons away. But let's not talk about that now," he said pensively.

The phone rang. It was a woman from the Asian Music Society in England. She had asked the orchestra to tour Britain in October with performances in London, Hull, Oxford, Manchester, and Birmingham. "You must come and hear us there," Xuan Ke said. I agreed I would.

While making tea, he talked about his family. His grandfather had been a traditional doctor who traveled by donkey from village to village with medicinal herbs. "He cured many people and also set broken bones," Xuan Ke said. Once his grandfather set the broken hand of a young boy and stayed on for a month at the boy's house to make sure it healed properly. Moved by the doctor's devotion, the boy's father gave his daughter to the doctor for a bride. Xuan Ke's grandfather accepted, and after the wedding the couple traveled together into Tibetan, Yi, Miao, and Pumi villages in the foothills of the Himalayas.

"During the Feast of the Full Moon in a Miao village, my father was born," Xuan Ke said. But when his father was twelve years old, he was abducted by a local leader and kept as a slave for ten years. When the slaveowner was taken ill, the boy called on his grandfather for help. The grandfather came and healed the slaveowner who, in return, gave the boy back to his parents.

By then Xuan Ke's father was twenty-two. While panning for gold near Tiger Leaping Gorge, where the Yangtze River sluices down a steep canyon a few miles north of Lijiang, he heard a woman singing. Her voice was so beautiful that he came back every day to listen. Finally, he convinced her to come to Lijiang with him. They traveled at night by horse and mule and carried a bag of gold dust. "When they arrived in Lijiang, he rented a house with the gold. This is the very house and this is where I was born," Xuan Ke said.

He stood up, a startled look on his face because we were coming to the part of the conversation he dreaded: his life in prison. Xuan Ke looked young and vigorous for his age, especially for a man who had lived through solitary confinement, repeated torture, and starvation, and who had been worked as hard as a draft horse during his healthy years.

It had begun to rain and the smell of mountain air slipped into the room as Xuan Ke put on a tape of Handel's *Water Music*. "Much of what I am has to do with Dr. Joseph Rock and the other foreigners who lived in Lijiang. They liked it here—the Dutch and Germans, Russians, and Americans. My father was hired to work for Joseph Rock in 1922 as a servant and guide, while Rock collected plants, studied the languages of the minorities, took notes on the Naxi religion and the *dongbas*—the shamans. Dr. Rock was very difficult, very bad tempered. He was famous for that, but he worked very hard."

After one year with Dr. Rock, Xuan Ke's father worked for the foreign missionaries in Lijiang. He cooked Western-style food and helped them in many ways since he spoke Tibetan, Yi, Mandarin, Naxi, and soon learned English, German, and some Dutch. He was the first Naxi to be sent to missionary school. The other villagers called him the "foreign slave." "Later they called me the foreign slave's son," Xuan Ke said, smiling.

In 1929 Xuan Ke's father guided an expedition to the Yunnan-Burma border. Theodore Roosevelt and his brother Kermit were in the hunting party and they shot a panther on the trip, the same expedition on which they killed a panda. The Roosevelts tipped Xuan Ke's father so well that he was considered a rich man. "That's when he built the second story on the house, the room where we are sitting. At the time it was the only two-story house in Lijiang."

Xuan Ke was christened and sent to missionary school where he was the only Naxi child. By age eleven, his English was so good he was enrolled in boarding school in Kunming. "There were ten pianos there," he remembered. "And many kinds of instruments. I had a good voice like my mother and the teachers told me I should become a musician. I studied piano, voice, then conducting. What I learned was mostly Western music. Later, I learned the ceremonial music of the Han Chinese which is what we now play." He looked out the window and smiled. "Come back and hear us again tonight. You may learn something more."

A hatch of flies broke out all over Lijiang the afternoon we tried to find Puji Monastery. Feng drove us through villages and wide fields where mares and foals grazed between women planting vegetables. The red clay roads, barely wide enough for one vehicle, were wet. We bumped up and up until the road became too narrow and treacherous, then walked the rest of the way. Si Wenfeng wasn't sure exactly where the monastery was. We climbed up dry canyons and crossed terraced fields past mule colts and the uneven, handmade adobe farmhouses whose roofs did not quite touch the tops of the walls.

In one village a row of trees curved around a house, making a garden wall of exposed roots. Another wall was made of brush threaded with wild rose. Baby chicks scattered everywhere at our feet and, at midday, cocks were crowing. The air was sultry—winter becoming spring becoming summer—and it drizzled warm rain. As we scrambled up a slope I mistook the repetitive cuckoo bird's call for a factory whistle. A band of horses grazed between village gardens and the beginning of steep foothills, and for the first time since arriving in China, I could breathe and feel and smell and hear.

From a thicket of shrubs we came on a high terraced field where two young men were working and asked the way to the monastery. "Up through there," they said, pointing to a forest of spindly trees. A pine wind blew all the flies away. In a clearing, an ancient wall contained a family graveyard, and the stones looked like small trees in the forest, growing slowly and silently for hundreds of years. Then we came to the outer wall of the temple.

The rain had turned frigid. The wall enclosed a tile-roofed temple complex dug into the side of a mountain. We followed it through trees, up hills, down the other side, but couldn't find a gate. Once, after I had fallen behind, I saw Zhang and Si embrace shyly but when I caught up, they were all business again. Finally we came on the entrance to the monastery: two red gates badly in need of paint creaked open. A sign over the entrance read *Daofu*—"good luck." The interior courtyard looked abandoned. Perhaps they meant to say, "Abandon hope all ye who enter here," as had been written at the entrance to the Tibetan monastery I'd once attended. In the corners of the covered entryway dried pea vines were piled to the ceiling, and beyond, two gnarled cherry trees graced the open courtyard flanked by pots of bonsai peach, pine, and palm. I looked up at a row of second-story windows but saw no faces; Zhang called out, but no one appeared.

Then rain came hard, splashing across each step to the temple. The outer ochre columns gave way to ones that were blood red, and blue and white knots of eternity decorated the corbels and rafters. I ran up the stairs and entered the meditation hall. One candle was burning, the flame convulsing sideways as rain on thin roof tiles shattered all other sound. Still no one appeared.

A wall of wooden doors, folded back on either side of the entrance, was painted with scenes of Buddhist stories and had been badly scratched. Inside, *tankas* (paintings) of great teachers and bodhisattvas hung from crumbling walls. I walked by empty incense braziers and faced the main altar, bent down and performed the requisite three prostrations, then turned on my heel. A wall of rain in the courtyard hid the old trees for a moment; their twisted arms showed through slowly as if to tell me with some weird botanic gesture how emptiness is formed, how silence is made, how formlessness is chiseled from form.

Two old caretakers appeared. "We have been sleeping," they reported quietly, because in the country it is normal for the Chinese to take a nap after the noon meal. From a narrow corridor the old lama appeared, barely five feet tall. He carried a toy-sized shovelful of embers and ashes and, nodding hello as he passed, proceeded to the incense burner, a rectangular bucket on three iron legs. In the residual ash he flattened an indentation that looked like a miniature caldera. Into this he dropped new embers, shaping them into the form of a mountain with the back of his tiny shovel, sprinking green powder on top, as if to represent trees. In a moment, the peak began smoldering.

When the rain began to let up we looked in toward the courtyard and saw the sky brighten. The lama said he cared for all the plants and trees, that the large trees, the *sakura* (cherry trees), were three hundred years old. From behind dripping eaves a curtain of gray storm clouds pulled apart to reveal the snowcapped mountains that separated Han China from Tibet.

When the lama was a young man, not yet twenty years old, he had walked alone to Lhasa in order to study the Dharma and said it had taken him three months to get there. Bandits stopped him all along the way but when they found he had nothing, owned nothing, they let him pass. He had come from a poor family and had to beg along the caravan trail. Sometimes when he was lonely and sad to have left his parents behind, he cheered himself with the knowledge that he would soon be in Lhasa, studying with a real Rinpoche, and that nothing else mattered.

He was now eighty-six years old and had come to this temple from Wenfeng Monastery fourteen years earlier because the resident lama there had died. "Now I will die here," he said. As he spoke the rain started again but more softly this time. He looked surprised when I told him I had studied with a Rinpoche and had spent a day with the sixteenth Karmapa (an important incarnate lama) when he visited the United States. The lama wasn't sure whether to believe me at first (the translation from Tibetan to Naxi to Chinese to English didn't help) but when I talked about the Karmapa's love of birds and his big aviary in India, the old lama started laughing, "Yes, yes . . . that is him, that is the same Karmapa."

He told me that he'd had visitors from Europe and the

United States who had studied Buddhism and even spoke and wrote Tibetan, though he couldn't imagine how the Dharma had gotten all the way over the ocean. I told him it went there the same way it got to China from India: by people on caravan routes who brought not just things, but ideas.

Before leaving, when I thought no one was looking, I did another three prostrations, then three more, and three more. Westerners find the idea of bowing down abhorrent, yet it's not bowing down at all, but rather exerting oneself physically to remove the mundane conditioning of consciousness and ego. I could have and should have continued all day.

The rain let up and when I stood I saw that the lama had been watching me. It was late afternoon and the shadow of the mountain behind the temple had swung over the monastery like a great cape or a carapace which I hoped might protect this place from future political ills. The lama said that during the Cultural Revolution, no one lived in the temple and they practiced at home very quietly. When I asked him what the scenes on the folding doors were, he said, scenes of Shambhala, the future Buddhist Shangri-la. The caretaker, who had once been a lama but had gotten married so that now he only worked there, began preparing for evening meditation. Reluctantly I turned to leave.

The storm had blown over but the darkness of late afternoon spread into the sky. We thanked them all and the caretakers closed the doors behind us. But when I looked back, the old lama was standing in the gate bowing over and over and I turned and bowed to him, walking backwards until I was in the pines, sliding downhill on fallen needles.

The next morning I ran into Xuan Ke in Lijaing's narrow lanes. It seemed impossible not to run into him; like a politician, he knew everyone and everyone knew him, but he wasn't running for office, only trying to resurrect a five-thousand-year-old culture in a very remote place. "Come to my house," he said, and I followed him up the creaking stairs to his study.

He closed the door, looked at me, then leaned very close, whispering: "Use soft words, please, when you write this. It is very important. Do you understand what I mean? My life could be in danger. Also, say that I thank Deng Xiaoping who gave me my freedom. I would not be alive today if it were not for him."

There was a silence, then he began: "I was in prison for twenty years. It began in 1948 when I was part of a student resistance group against the Kuomintang, fighting for more democracy. But I was so stupid. I could not lie. I stated openly that I was a member and there were spies among the students, so quite soon I was caught and sent to prison for three months. I was seventeen years old and when my father found out where I was, he got someone from the church to write a letter saying: 'Please let him go. He is so young and naive.' I got out. The missionaries from the conservatory begged me not to join again. They offered to send me to California to become a great conductor. But I joined again, this time one of the groups operating in the mountains, called the forest army. I was caught again.

"When Mao took over I was released and went back to Kunming. I became the conductor of an orchestra. We had to play revolutionary music but I always added Western music and rewrote Chinese music with Western harmonies. I became known and began writing articles and music reviews. Always honest. And so, my reputation grew. But high trees catch a lot of wind, the old proverb goes.

"Some things happened and I needed money, so I asked my sister who lived in Calcutta, her husband was Tibetan and was an aide to the Dalai Lama. This was now 1958. A cousin in Hong Kong sent me cash via the Bank of China. I did not know this was the bank that funneled money to the Kuomintang spies. The police came around and forced me to give addresses of my relatives. I refused. So they put me in prison and gave me nothing to eat. Days went by. They did not believe my story about the money. Finally I gave them some addresses, but that was not enough. They wanted names of other people. I was very scared. After I gave them some names, they set me free, but I was not allowed to leave Kunming and my reviews were no longer published. Everything Western—music, songs, and opinions—was prohibited. Mao went around asking all the artists and intellectuals to criticize his government, to help him make it better. We thought he was the second coming of Christ and so we did as we were told. But he betrayed us. Those of us who spoke our minds were punished. It was his clever way of purging the country of enemies so that he could do anything he wanted without dissent. At a meeting of artists I spoke out and said: 'Do you want to see a wall? Go out into the street and even in daylight take a lamp with you, because there is darkness at noon.' After that, I was labeled a rightist.

"Soon after, I was put in prison again. I'd had a love affair with a singer. She wasn't very good but she was ambitious, and she denounced me to the authorities. I went to prison for seven years, this time on the Vietnamese border in a tin mine. My father was also in prison because of his contacts with the Western missionaries. He died in prison in 1959. I never saw him all those years.

"One day a guard asked me if I could paint. I couldn't, but I said yes. I was told to paint eleven communist leaders—Marx, Mao, Engels, Chou En-lai. I got a better room and was allowed to go to town for supplies. Everyone was happy for me. They put up their thumbs. When I was finished with the paintings one of the prisoners who was a spy asked me which one was the hardest to paint and I said, Marx, because of his hair and beard.

"Three days later all three thousand prisoners were ordered to stand outside. Guards in six watchtowers were armed with machine guns. There were police dogs, then the commander asked the spy who had talked to me about the painting to repeat what I, a bad man, had said about the greatest leader on earth, Marx. He told the story.

"'Is it true?' they asked me. I said yes. They came behind me and held my arms so tight I thought they had been dislocated. They said I hated Marx, asked me to admit it. I screamed, 'No, that's not what I meant. I was just talking about a technical problem.' But the prisoners started screaming, 'Beat him! Xuan Ke is a wicked man!'

"When the guards produced a rope, someone said it wasn't good enough, that they must use the wire rope, which they brought out, and they hung me by the wrists. The skin burst. Blood came out. My hands blackened. I do not know how long I hung there in the sun because I lost consciousness after a while. When I came round I was lying on a plank bed. Flies covered my hands and I had no power to chase them off. After, I could never use my right arm properly again.

"I lay in bed for a year. No strength to work. A doctor told me to practice piano in the air with my hands to make them strong, but it didn't work. The next year I had to work in a coal mine. I had a gas lamp on my head because it was dark and dangerous. There were many casualties, many deaths down there. I had good musical ears and when I heard something wrong in the mines I warned everyone, and by this I saved many.

"The next year the political climate improved a little. I was told that if anything was wrong I should report it. I said I had been unfairly accused of contacting the Dalai Lama. But I was not allowed to say that they were wrong and I was right, so I got an extra three years.

"One night I talked in my sleep, in English. In the morning I was accused of practicing English during the night, implying that I wanted to escape. For this I was taken away and beaten. They locked me in an isolation cell for seven months. There were forty-two little ventilation holes in the cement under the wall. The cell was 1.2 square meters. At night, water dripped on my head. I begged the guards to do something but they just laughed. 'That is your own sweat,' they said. Some prisoners went blind in those cells. That is why I rubbed my eyes with the water.

"All those days I practiced breathing slowly. I prayed and meditated and hummed music to myself. Also I sang a Naxi song, "Wo Tzu," to scare away the demons. Sometimes the sun glimmered through the holes and I could see the mountains. I counted the trees. I believed that if all the trees remained standing I had nothing to fear, but if one of them should fall over things would turn out badly for me. I received only vegetables and rice once a day. After the meal I thought about the future. I wanted to return to Lijiang, get married, write. I thought about music, about the sacred music that had helped keep me alive.

"When those seven months were over I had to work in a factory where we washed tin. In 1975 an order came from Beijing. Mao said that prisoners were not to be beaten any longer and we had to be paid. We would now be rehabilitated into proper workers. Everybody was happy. The factory was no longer guarded although our freedom of movement was limited. I had met a young woman from the village nearby and wanted to get married. Some of her relatives were also in prison and they thought I was too old—I was 45 and she was 19. But finally we were given a leave to get married.

"In 1977, when the Gang of Four was disbanded most of us were set free. But freedom didn't come to much in those days. I had already lost twenty-one years of freedom. I got a job in a nearby sawmill but still had to report to the authorities regularly. In the evenings I taught English, which was a great success, and later I got a teaching certificate. My wife and I moved back to Lijiang. At first I rented a house, just like my father, and spent all my time in the library, studying Taoist and Dongba scriptures and thinking about the purpose of sacred music.

"During those seven months in solitary confinement I realized that all singing and music arose from fear, the fear of death. In the Stone Age people believed that spirits devoured the body after death—also real wild animals devoured the living—so these had to be chased away. Ksj, ksj, ksj! Go, go! That's what the songs say, and with them, wild gesticulations. From these arose songs and dance.

"Now I spend my life of freedom thinking about these things, studying the early music of China, Tibet, and of the Naxi. This early music still has the form and content of the first songs. There are sounds in this music to chase away demons, to chase away tigers. In the Naxi language, the word for fear sounds almost like the word for spirit. I think they are the same."

Xuan Ke suddenly looked at his watch. "Oh, I have forgotten. The ten of us who are going to London on tour have to go to the hospital for medical exams. Could you give me a ride?"

We wound through the tangled streets of Lijiang and entered the courtyard of the hospital. Inside, the orchestra members were lined up in chairs, all smiling. Xuan Ke introduced me. "She is going to come to London." They all nodded and smiled: Hao, hao . . . yes, yes. "On October 8th. . . ." Then a nurse whisked him away.

From

Tian Wen

or

Questions

of Heaven

17

What is the particular virtue of the moon, the Brightness of
the Night, which causes it to grow once more after its death?
Of what advantage is it to keep a toad in the belly?

21

What is it whose closing causes the dark and whose opening
causes the light? Where does the Bright God hide before the
Horn proclaims the dawning of the day?

V

LONDON

"These rooms must be for an empress," the old paper cutter said of the Kensington hotel that had been arranged for Xuan Ke and the orchestra during their tour in London. It was October and I had just arrived to see them perform. The frail old artisan who couldn't have weighed more than eighty pounds, sank slowly onto the couch. "I have never sat on such a chair before!" he exclaimed. "It is like a cloud!"

Only ten players from the orchestra's thirty-three had come on tour. They had arrived three days earlier and were still trying to understand that jet lag was not the same as sickness. Except for Xuan Ke, who had once performed in Beijing, none of them had ever traveled out of their province, none had used any form of transportation except bicycle, car, and horse cart, none had seen the inside of a plane, none had ever eaten anything but Chinese food.

The young woman, Huang Limei, showed me around a living room, kitchen, and four bedrooms, the biggest of which was used for rehearsing. "And the bathrooms . . . we've never seen so many bathrooms," she said, wide eyed. Long underwear hung to dry over the shower curtain. She whispered, "The old men had to be shown how to use the toilets. They didn't know."

We sat down in the living room and the young flutist brought me tea. "From Lijiang," he said proudly, pointing to the two trunks filled with food they had lugged from home. They had asked for rooms with a kitchen so they could cook for themselves. How did you like the airplane? I asked the paper cutter. Did it frighten you? He looked straight at me, then shook his head calmly. "It was very nice . . . but landing . . . it hurt my ears."

Xuan Ke sat on the couch opposite. "We are afraid of nothing! Except the food," he announced enthusiastically. The drummer chimed in, "We tried to eat a sandwich yesterday . . . oh, my . . . it was terrible. We had to spit it out!"

The Asian Music Association, which had sponsored their trip to London, had taken them sightseeing. "The air is so good here, there is no dust in the streets, but we think there are more cars than people! So strange. And also, those cars are very orderly. They must have many rules . . . oh, that would be hard to learn," the accountant said.

"We liked Buckingham Palace," the poet said. "We didn't know people ever lived like that. But everyone in London so busy. So hurry. We have expression in Lijiang: Everyone after birth will go to place called Death so why go quickly? We from Lijiang enjoy life. Not like Japanese time—always running. Why go to that place in hurry? We don't understand. That's why our music is slow. It is how a man does his walking."

A jar of Yunnan chilies sat on the coffee table along with Chinese cigarettes and matches. "You even brought matches?" I asked. "We didn't know if they had matches here," came the reply. The accountant, He Linghan, the Communist Party secretary, He Jiaxiu, and the scholar, Yang Zenglie, sat with us while the poet and drummer finished washing breakfast dishes.

Visitors arrived; the door was always left open. "That's our policy in Lijiang," Xuan Ke said smiling. It was an Austrian chemist who had lived in Lijiang with his Chinese wife while translating Chinese pharmacology texts into German. He had come to buy one of the scrolls Xuan Ke had brought. A trunk was opened and twenty or thirty paintings were unwound on the floor—landscapes in the traditional style, though none of them more than a hundred years old.

My London friend Anxi, who promised to translate for me, came in carrying bags of groceries from Chinatown. From Beijing, she was a teenager during the Cultural Revolution and had been forced to join the Red Guards, disrupting her studies to become a concert pianist. She is now married to a British film director. Though she hadn't known Xuan Ke before, anyone from China is considered a friend by the Chinese music community in London. Gregarious and funny, she had endeared herself to the musicians as soon as they arrived and now they carried on like old friends.

"I was in Lijiang during the Cultural Revolution when I was in a Red Guard brigade," she said. "It was the first time I had seen that part of China. Everyone was so poor. They had been poor before Liberation, and they remained poor after."

The Communist Party secretary, who was part of the orchestra and had been purposely sent on tour to keep watch over the others, listened to Anxi and said: "Before the revolution Lijiang had rich people: merchants who did big business in India and Tibet. Many shops, many traders, and two landlords with big holdings. Everyone else was poor. Seventy percent of the people were poor. The change in 1949 was very important."

Sun Ziming, the old paper cutter, still savoring the softness of the couch, said, "It was hard to get food, hard to get any money at all. Every day my father sent me to the mountains to get firewood to sell. If it didn't sell, we didn't eat. People in the mountains are still poor, still no school, no medicine. Can't write. Now I am building a new house with my sons and grandsons outside of town. After 1949, everything got better. Now four generations of us all live together."

"They are an army!" Xuan Ke said, laughing and standing to leave.

By afternoon the musicians were exhausted from trying to make sense of the streets, shops, and traffic, and opted to stay in their hotel room, much as I had often done in China. They padded around in stocking feet drinking tea and writing in their journals, the kind used by schoolchildren. Others wrote postcards home, the scholar writing postcards for the ones who were illiterate. They took turns scrutinizing the pictures on the front of the cards, trying to understand what they were seeing. I asked if they were homesick and they shook their heads. "In the postcards we said we are all right, but it will take ten days for the mail to get there and by then, we'll be home."

The fat accountant sat with his pants rolled up to his shins and his shirt hanging out over his potbelly. London was having a heat wave and the temperature soared to eighty. They asked if it was always this hot here, as we opened all the windows.

While the butcher and drummer began preparing lunch, the accountant seemed to doze. But when I inquired about his music he jerked awake and spoke passionately. "I began when I was twelve years old and from age sixteen, I played music with the master in my village. We made our own instruments—bamboo flutes, and necks for lutes, and snakeskin covers for drums. In 1949, all this stopped, but in the early sixties we started again, only to be stopped during the Cultural Revolution. But all the time, I loved music as much as I loved food," he said, patting his lopsided potbelly and laughing. "Just recently, I finally retired from my accounting job, but I grew bored—even the music wasn't enough—so I started working again, but when this tour was offered, I quit so I could come to London."

When I asked if he was glad he had come, he smiled slowly, checked to see if the Communist secretary was listening, then said, "Yes, yes. Now I know better who I am."

I heard the little bamboo flute piping and looked up to see the butcher dancing around the room like a *wu* shaman. He had emerged from the kitchen with hands dripping. "I belong to the school of music and laughter," the young butcher said. "I'm not a religious man." He was jaunty with a stocky build, and his cheap serge suit was pulled tightly across his chest because the buttons had been sewn on wrong, making the front of the jacket lopsided; the label was still sewn onto the coat sleeve.

The scholar closed his eyes and sat up straight, then peered at me with intelligent eyes and a calm demeanor. "The music we play is not complicated. It's easy. What's hard is the traditional style, because it is mostly forgotten. It's the feeling of the music, what's inside of it, because it's not folk music, not about something—it's religious music, so the feeling must be embodied by the musician or it won't sound right. We realized this after the Cultural Revolution. The old people still remember in their hearts all the music, so I go to them and listen. There are still some alive. In other areas, the old people were killed or died during the Cultural Revolution, but not in Lijiang. Even so, we have waited too long." Having studied the clarinet at the conservatory, the scholar was now dedicated to helping Xuan Ke with ethnomusicology research. Without explanation, he stood and sang a Dongba funeral song.

After lunch the musicians took naps, leaving me sipping tea in the living room. Anxi, who had been translating for me in Xuan Ke's absence, took me to a Chinese grocery store to buy food for the evening meal. "We must feed them while they are here," she said. "They have so little." We picked through bins of vegetables: bok choy and long beans, bitter melon, and assorted greens. The night before we had been to dinner at a Chinese restaurant and Anxi had scowled at the food. "This isn't real Chinese food," she reported. But when the musicians cooked for us—the simplest fare with no sauces, just chilies sprinkled over everything—Anxi smiled. "This tastes like home," she purred.

At the butcher case she ordered meat, speaking to the man in Mandarin and to me in English. "It is so complex . . . the mind of the Chinese," she said, pointing at pork ribs. "Because of the way our social history has disciplined us and made us believe strongly in things. So when the Chairman came in the very beginning, we loved him. We believed we were struggling for the people, that we could change."

Standing at the checkout counter she continued. "I was twelve and thirteen during the Great Leap Forward. I worked at a furnace in Beijing. I hadn't been living with my parents for a long time. Families were divided up and children were sent to work camps. We took everything metal. We stole anything we saw to put in the furnace, then our Red Guard unit stood on top of the roofs and waved red flags for everyone to see. We had achieved our goal—we didn't know then that the steel we made was useless. During that time we stopped going to school. That's when the farmers left everything in the fields to work at the furnaces and the worms came up from the ground and ate everything. I had to stop my piano studies then. I was meant to be a concert pianist, but it was no longer possible. In this way I am like Xuan Ke. We were both meant to become musicians but that time was lost to us. Now we are too old."

Back at the hotel, Xuan Ke had returned and was practicing his speech for the evening performance. When Anxi asked how he felt about the future of music in China, Xuan Ke said, "The world has changed into a better place. I'm talking about China. That is the world to us. I am protected now; I am safe. If I disappeared, the world would know that things were bad again."

We talked about the healing power of music, how, when I had been very ill I had played the music of Kevin Volans, whose string quartets Bruce Chatwin had played when he was dying, music Bruce had sent to Xuan Ke too. "Yes, music can restore the balance and harmony of the world, if our bodies learn how to be receptive to it," Xuan Ke said.

The old paper cutter sat down with us. He was revered by the others in the orchestra. "His was a very traditional art in China," Xuan Ke said. "The scissors he used to make his cutouts were this small," he said, holding out his little finger, and halving it. "It was very meticulous work. Not many could do it."

When I asked the old man if he believed in the healing power of music, he laughed at first, then suddenly grew serious. "I forget everything when I play. All my heart goes into the music. If I don't concentrate, the music changes, so it's best to forget all distractions and just play."

At that moment music began. The other players had begun rehearsing in an adjacent bedroom. Tonight would be their first concert in the prestigious Purcell Room at the South Bank Centre. "We went yesterday for a sound rehersal. We have never seen such a room. But I do not know if our Naxi music will be the same there. It has never been played outside of China. Perhaps it will not travel well," Xuan Ke said.

The hall was sold out. As the audience quieted, the musicians walked onstage, transformed by Tang Dynasty costumes. The men wore silk brocade tunics in black and gold over long crimson skirts, and the young woman wore traditional Naxi dress, a white aproned skirt and a deep red vest. Carrying their ancient instruments, they took their seats. The drummer and butcher who had washed the morning dishes together were now sitting side by side. "We play with wisdom, not expertise; we play with heart," Xuan Ke had said earlier. Now he came onstage looking humble at first, then sprightly and young for his sixty-six years. His Taoist priest's long blue robe touched the tops of scuffed loafers. He had on mismatched turquoise socks.

Blinking in the hard theatre lights, Xuan Ke began: "We come from the foot of the Himalayas to bring you sacred music of Taoism from the Tang Dynasty. This music used to be all of China's. They lost it. Now it is ours and we call it Naxi music. We are from a remote place but it is full of culture. We are preserving a tradition that is thousands of years old and we are happy to bring it to you now in this faraway place called London."

After introducing the musicians, he stepped forward holding two four-hundred-year-old hand cymbals from Tibet and asked everyone to be very quiet. A clear ringing shivered through the theatre as if the room were a pond and a thrown stone had caused concentric circles to radiate out. Xuan Ke smiled impishly. "Good? . . . We like it." Then he rang a gong and the music began.

That night the Naxi music sounded like mountains and rivers and reefs of clouds diving and filling the Yangtze River Valley, streaming out of Tiger Leaping Gorge where Xuan Ke's mother once sang, casting a green spell on Jade Mountain Peak where clouds are made, causing them to rain down rain and snow and more music.

The players were nervous and once during the evening the old paper cutter forgot which tune they were to begin. When he picked up the wrong instrument, the scholar leaned over, patiently took the lute out of his hands and faced him toward the cloud gongs. Later in the evening the scholar started swallowing hard—his nervousness had caused thirst—but when the new song began, he sat up straight, closed his eyes and played, transported by the music he had helped bring back to life. At the end there was a standing ovation.

After the performance a well-known concert pianist from China who had been a conservatory student with Xuan Ke came backstage to see his old friend. "I haven't seen him for forty-three years," Xuan Ke had told me. "It was in Kunming when I was the conductor of a choir and he was the pianist."

They embraced and when a news photographer set off his flash, I saw tears in Xuan Ke's eyes. The pianist had been sent from China to study piano in the United States, and after winning the Chopin Competition, had returned to Kunming to see his parents. It happened to be the eve of Mao's Hundred Flowers purge, and the pianist's parents had both committed suicide that morning. When the young musician heard this news he knew he had to escape and immediately made his way to Hong Kong, then to London, never to return.

The two men sat alone in a far corner of the room and talked head-to-head for a long time while other well-wishers filed in and out. Later, Xuan Ke pulled me aside and whispered: "He offered me a job and a place to live here in London. But I would have to stay when the tour was over, not go back. I couldn't do that. I would never see my family again, and they would be in danger. I have set out to preserve what's left of our culture. No one else will do it. I must go home."

In the morning I went to their hotel to say good-bye. Every conversation I'd had with the musicians revealed how concerned they were with the Confucian ideal of the societal "I." Xuan Ke was going home to work for the good of China, just as Anxi had done under Mao, just as Confucius did while writing the *Analects*. In medieval China, travel, and the paintings and writings that sprang from it, functioned as a mirror of the moral self and represented a panoramic, all-encompassing view of reality, of natural and human meaning.

I thought of the old lama at Puji Monastery in the foothills of Lijiang carrying incense ashes from his room to the burner outside the meditation hall. How slowly and carefully he shaped them into a mountain topped with green on which hermits lived and pavilions were built, the summit crowned by gleaming temples. As the embers ignited, the whole mountain blazed to burn away confusion and ignorance—I watched them crumble—and as pilgrims trooped up its steep slopes an old man with a broom appeared, sweeping away all our tracks and fears.

In the hotel room, Xuan Ke sat in a chair by the window. He looked subdued; he was still brooding over his visit with his pianist friend. Cigarette smoke swirled above his head like bad weather. He reminded me of Chieh Yu, the Madman of Chu, an ancient draft dodger who feigned madness to avoid state service and went off to the slopes of Emei Shan with his wife and child to live as a hermit. There is no such thing in Chinese society as "loyal opposition"—Xuan Ke found that out the hard way. The Madman's motto was: "To obey, but resist. That is the whole secret."

Xuan Ke greeted me and thrummed my little notebook. "Remember, use soft words," he said. "There is still danger for all of us." The butcher brought a big bowl of congee from the kitchen, stopping midstep to play a song on the bamboo pipe that had been sticking out of his back pocket. He was still high from the success of the concert, from the glories of travel away from home.

Xuan Ke leaned toward me and showed me his teeth: "My wife keeps asking me to get my teeth fixed. They are all bad since being in prison. But they are like the Great Wall; the history of my life and therefore the history of the Chinese people shows in them, so they will stay like this," he said.

Ignoring the food, Xuan Ke lit another cigarette, but now he was smiling. "In China too many people behave the same. All blue suits in Mao's time. Now, it's all karaoke . . . but I act different always. I have dangerous lips. I talk too much. Honesty is the only way anyone will know what is the real history and I will always tell it."

We dished out rice and eggs into bowls and dropped hot Yunnan chilies on top. As the butcher played an eerie, melancholy tune on the pipe, Xuan Ke wiggled his darkened teeth. "Remember these," he said, his eyes sparkling.

Bibliography

Birnbaum, Raoul. "Buddhist Encounters with the Wutai Mountains." 1995 (unpublished).

——"The Real Face and the True Form: Medieval Buddhist Representations of Dieties and Mountains." Paper delivered at the University of California at Santa Barbara, 1993.

Bush, Susan, and Hsio-yen Shih. *Early Chinese Texts on Painting*. Cambridge: Harvard-Yenching Institute, 1985.

Chan, Wing-Tsit. *A Source Book in Chinese Philosophy*. Princeton, N.J.: Princeton University Press, 1963.

Chatwin, Bruce. *What Am I Doing Here*. New York: Viking, 1989.

Cheng, Francois. *Empty and Full*. Boston: Shambhala Publications, 1994.

Cleary, Thomas. *Practical Taoism*. Boston: Shambhala Publications, 1996.

De Bary, William Theodore. *Sources of Chinese Tradition*, vol. 1. New York: Columbia University Press, 1960.

Egan, Ronald. *Word, Image and Deed in the Life of Su Shi*.

Cambridge: Harvard-Yenching Institute, Harvard University Press, 1994.

Fairbank, John. *China*. Cambridge: Harvard University Press, 1992.

Gernet, Jacques. *Daily Life in China*. Stanford, Calif.: Stanford University Press, 1962.

Goullart, Peter. *Forgotten Kingdom*. London: John Murry, 1957.

Hargett, James M. "Literary Visions of Mount Emei during the Tang and Song." Paper delivered at the University of California at Santa Barbara, 1993.

Hartman, Charles. "Mountains as Metaphors in Tang Religious Texts and the Northern Landscape Painting of the Tenth Century." Paper delivered at the University of California at Santa Barbara, 1993.

Hawkes, David, trans. *The Songs of the South*. New York: Penguin Books, 1985.

Kinohata, Kiyohiko. *Sacred Mountains in Chinese Art*. Urbana, Ill.: University of Illinois Press, 1991.

Kristof, Nicolas D. and Wudun, Sheryl. *China Wakes*. New York: Vintage Books, 1995.

Naquin, Susan, and Chun-Fang Yu. *Pilgrims and Sacred Sites in China*. Berkeley, Calif.: University of California Press, 1992.

Polo, Marco. *Travels*. New York: Penguin Books, 1958.

Porter, Bill. *Road to Heaven*. San Francisco: Mercury House, 1993.

Rock, Joseph. *The Ancient Na-Khi Kingdom of Southwest China*. Cambridge: Harvard University Press, 1947.

Schaller, George. *The Last Panda*. Chicago: University of Chicago Press, 1993.

Spence, Jonathan. *The Gate of Heavenly Peace*. New York: Penguin, 1981.

Strassberg, William. *Inscribed Landscape*. Berkeley, Calif.: University of California Press, 1994.

Sullivan, Michael. *Chinese Landscape Painting*. Berkeley, Calif.: University of California Press, 1980.

Tuchman, Barbara. *Stilwell and the American Experience in China*. New York: The Macmillan Company, 1970.

Watson, Burton, trans. *Chuang Tzu*. New York: Columbia University Press, 1968.

———. *The Columbia Book of Chinese Poetry*. New York: Columbia University Press, 1984.

———. *Early Chinese Literature*. New York: Columbia University Press, 1962.

———. *Selected Poems of Su Tung-p'o*. Port Townsend, Wash.: Copper Canyon Press, 1994.

Welch, Homes. *The Practice of Chinese Buddhism*. Cambridge: Harvard University Press, 1967.

Wright, Arthur F. *Buddhism in Chinese History*. Stanford, Calif.: Stanford University Press, 1959.

Xianliang, Zhang. *Grass Soup*. London: Minerva, 1994.

Yeats, W. B. *The Poems*. New York: Macmillan Publishing Co., 1983.

Zhisui, Li. *The Private Life of Chairman Mao*. New York: Random House, 1994.

BIBLIOGRAPHY

Credits

"Bell and Drum on the South River Bank" and "From the traveler, singing" from *Selected Poems of Su Tung-p'o*, translated by Burton Watson. Copyright © 1994 by Burton Watson. Reprinted by permission of Copper Canyon Press.

Questions from *Tian Wen*, quoted in *The Songs of the South: An Ancient Chinese Anthology of Poems by Qu Yuan and Other Poets*, translated by David Hawkes. Copyright © 1985 by David Hawkes. Reprinted by permission of Penguin Books Ltd.

CREDITS

Library of Congress Cataloging-in-Publication Data

Ehrlich, Gretel.

Questions of heaven : the Chinese journeys of an American
Buddhist / Gretel Ehrlich.

p. cm. — (Concord library)

ISBN 0-8070-7310-5 (cloth)

ISBN 0-8070-7311-3 (paper)

1. Ehrlich, Gretel—Journeys—China. 2. China—Description
and travel. I. Title. II. Series.

PS3555.H72A3 1997

818'.5403—dc21

[B] 96-45518